exploring

HEAVENLY PLACES

Miracles on the Mountain of the Lord

VOLUME 6

Give thanks to the Lord and proclaim his greatness. Let the whole world know what he has done. (1 Chronicles 16:8)

Rob Gross

EXPLORING HEAVENLY PLACES, VOLUME 6
Miracles on the Mountain of the Lord

By Rob Gross

Aslan's Place Publications
9315 Sagebrush Street
Apple Valley, CA 92308
760-810-0990
www.aslansplace.com

All Rights Reserved. No part of this book may be reproduced or transmitted in any form or by any means—electronic or mechanical, including photocopying, recording, or by any information storage and retrieval system—without written permission from the authors except as provided by the copyright laws of the United States of America. Unauthorized reproduction is a violation of federal and spiritual laws.

English Standard Version (ESV): The Holy Bible, English Standard Version Copyright © 2001 by Crossway Bibles, a publishing ministry of Good News Publishers.

New American Standard Bible (NASB): Copyright © 1960, 1962, 1963, 1968, 1971, 1972, 1973, 1975, 1977, 1995 by The Lockman Foundation

New International Version (NIV): Holy Bible, New International Version®, NIV® Copyright ©1973, 1978, 1984, 2011 by Biblica, Inc.® Used by permission. All rights reserved worldwide.

New King James Version (NKJV): Scripture taken from the New King James Version®. Copyright © 1982 by Thomas Nelson. Used by permission. All rights reserved.

New Living Translation (NLT): *Holy Bible*, New Living Translation, copyright © 1996, 2004, 2015 by Tyndale House Foundation. Used by permission of Tyndale House Publishers Inc., Carol Stream, Illinois 60188. All rights reserved.

Greek definitions are derived from *Strong's Greek Concordance*
http://biblehub.com/concordance/

Hebrew definitions are derived from *Strong's Hebrew Concordance*
http://biblehub.com/concordance/

Copyright 2016, by Rob Gross
All rights reserved.
Editor: Barbara Kain Parker
Cover Design: Brodie Schmidtke
ISBN # 978-1-5136-2483-9
Printed in the United States of America

I dedicate this book to my wife, Barbara, who has helped facilitate healing in my life in a myriad of ways.

TABLE OF CONTENTS

FOREWARD 6
INTRODUCTION 7
CHAPTER 1: *The Lord of the Breakthrough* 10
CHAPTER 2: *The Pathway to Healing* 13
CHAPTER 3: *I Want My Church Back* 22
CHAPTER 4: *Revival, Revolution, Reformation* 28
CHAPTER 5: *From Orphans to Sons and Daughters* 34
CHAPTER 6: *Miracles on the Mountain of the Lord* 39
CHAPTER 7: *Anxiety, Fear and Stress* 44
CHAPTER 8: *Miracles at Macy's* 47
CHAPTER 9: *Test Me Again—I'm Healed!* 53
CHAPTER 10: *Set Free from the Ungodly Depth* 55
CHAPTER 11: *Friendship Evangelism* 63
CHAPTER 12: *A Dramatic Twist* 68
CHAPTER 13: *Handkerchiefs, Aprons, and Folded Paper* .. 70
CHAPTER 14: *Cancer—Gone!* 73
CHAPTER 15: *Jumping for Joy* 78
CHAPTER 16: *High Blood Pressure Healed* 80
CHAPTER 17: *Ominous Spot Disappears* 84
CHAPTER 18: *The Pain is Gone!* 87
CHAPTER 19: *Mailbox Wonders* 89
CHAPTER 20: *Massive Brain Aneurysm Healed* 91
CHAPTER 21: *Asthma Healed* 93
CHAPTER 22: *Ears Opened* 96
CHAPTER 23: *God Loves Hindus* 98

CHAPTER 24: *Migraine Miracles* 99
CHAPTER 25: *God Heals Through Us—In Spite of Us!* 102
CHAPTER 26: *A Buddhist Couple Turns to Jesus* 105
CHAPTER 27: *Children Do Not Have a 'Junior' Holy Spirit* 107
CHAPTER 28: *The Fireman's Boot* 109
CHAPTER 29: *Miracle on Maui* 112
CHAPTER 30: *Barren No More* 117
CHAPTER 31: *Unexpected Breakthroughs* 119
CHAPTER 32: *Rescued Off the Beach* 125
CHAPTER 33: *Miracle at the Farmer's Market* 128
CHAPTER 34: *Long Term Recovery Miracle* 130
CHAPTER 35: *Dimensional Breakthroughs* 132
CHAPTER 36: *The Power of Desperate Prayer* 138
CHAPTER 37: *Until…* 142
CHAPTER 38: *Closing Thoughts* 149
APPENDIX: *Have You Received Jesus?* 154
GLOSSARY 155
ABOUT THE AUTHOR 160

FOREWARD

"Where's the beef?" I cannot imagine how many times I have said that over the past several years. The classic phrase originated with a Wendy's commercial from 1984, and was made famous by actress Clara Peller. To me it means, "Where is the evidence?" Why would I say that? Because I want to see tangible results of healing from the utilizing in ministry the revelation we have been shown by the Lord. He has heard my request! Not long ago, I was talking to a friend who did not know of my private conversations with the Lord about 'the beef' when he turned to me and said, "The Lord just told me to tell you that He is going to show you the beef." The truth is, the Lord is showing us the beef, and this book is part of it.

Rob Gross, the senior pastor of Mountain View Community Church in Kaneohe, Hawaii, is constantly implementing the revelation the Lord gives us about the heavenly places, as he trains people how to minister to others. *Exploring Heavenly Places, Miracles on the Mountain of the Lord* contains many testimonies of how healing has taken place by utilizing revelation not only from Aslan's Place but also from many other ministries. The book contains stories of real and lasting healing as well as teachings on how to implement Biblical revelation in ministry to others. This is not a how-to book but rather, teaches how we can "do what the Father is doing"[1] as Jesus did. Rob is convinced that the Kingdom of God is not just a matter of talk but of Power—God's Power.[2] You are about to read true stories of people who have been touched by the Power of God. Get ready to have your faith stirred to believe that church no longer has to be conformed to business as usual.

[1] John 5:19

[2] Read more about the Power of God in *Exploring Heavenly Places, Power in the Heavenly Places* and *Exploring Heavenly Places, God's Power, On Earth as it is in Heaven* (volumes 4 and 5).

INTRODUCTION

Throughout the Bible we read wonderful Scriptures that declare the wondrous power of God to heal:

> *The Spirit of the Lord is upon me, for he has anointed me to bring Good News to the poor. He has sent me to proclaim that captives will be released, that the blind will see, that the oppressed will be set free, and that the time of the Lord's favor has come.*[1]

> *And you know that God anointed Jesus of Nazareth with the Holy Spirit and with power. Then Jesus went around doing good and healing all who were oppressed by the devil, for God was with him.*[2]

> *I tell you the truth, anyone who believes in me will do the same works I have done, and even greater works, because I am going to be with the Father.*[3]

> *[Jesus said,] "These miraculous signs will accompany those who believe: They will cast out demons in my name, and they will speak in new languages. They will be able to handle snakes with safety, and if they drink anything poisonous, it won't hurt them. They will be able to place their hands on the sick, and they will be healed." And the disciples went everywhere and preached, and the Lord worked through them, confirming what they said by many miraculous signs.*[4]

> *But the believers who were scattered preached the Good News about Jesus wherever they went. Philip, for example, went to the city of Samaria and told the people there about the Messiah. Crowds listened intently to Philip because they were eager to hear his message and see the miraculous signs he did. Many evil spirits were cast out, screaming as they left their victims. And many who had been paralyzed or lame were healed. So there was great joy in that city.*[5]

> *Are any of you suffering hardships? You should pray. Are any of you happy? You should sing praises. Are any of you sick? You should call for the elders of the church to come and pray over you, anointing you with oil in the name of the Lord. Such a prayer*

offered in faith will heal the sick, and the Lord will make you well. And if you have committed any sins, you will be forgiven.[6]

For the earnest expectation of the creation eagerly waits for the revealing of the sons of God.[7]

How often have we read such words of hope for and wondered how they apply today because almost everywhere we look someone is sick with something? Well, there's good news because:

Jesus Christ is the same yesterday, today, and forever.[8]

Still, some may ask, "Where is there evidence that God's miraculous power is for today?" This volume in the *Exploring Heavenly Places* series answers that question with documented instances in which God has moved through His people, His revealed sons and daughters, to minister to others. You will read how:

- Healing broke out during a Sunday morning worship service as God moved through the members of the congregation, and not just the pastor
- A woman diagnosed with a 95% blockage in her arteries received a clean bill of health from the doctor after receiving prayer from her mail carrier
- A high school baseball coach died of a heart attack at a game and was raised from the dead
- A young man with a sexually transmitted disease was healed after asking for prayer
- An entire high school baseball team received Christ
- People suffering from arthritis were powerfully delivered
- A 10-year-old girl with bi-polar disease was set free
- The deaf can now hear
- Stage 4 lung cancer was miraculously healed
- A woman miraculously recovered after a massive brain aneurysm although the doctor gave her no chance of survival

Yes, God is still in the business of setting people free physically, emotionally and spiritually. There is no aspect of our being, whether body, soul or spirit where His healing touch cannot penetrate.

Miracles On the Mountain of the Lord is a compilation of real life stories about everyday people who have prayed for others, and then witnessed their recovery. If you are dealing with a life threatening or debilitating disease, this book will give you hope that God can heal you too. If you are a believer and you know that there's more to Church than just Sunday attendance at a church[9] facility, this book is also for you. If you feel called to heal the sick and set captives free, this book will not only encourage you to repeatedly cross the chicken line as prompted by the Holy Spirit, but will also give you a glimpse of some of the new things God has been revealing and releasing to His Body to empower you for greater kingdom impact.

Radical change is in the air. A new move of God is knocking at our doorstep. Fasten your seat belts because God is about to take the Church on a supernaturally natural ride. This ride does not have an unknown destination, but is a return trip to our original design.[10]

---

[1] Luke 4:18-19 NLT

[2] Acts 10:38 NLT

[3] John 14:12 NLT

[4] Mark 16:17-18 NLT

[5] Acts 8:4-8 NLT

[6] James 5:13-15 NLT

[7] Romans 8:19 NKJV

[8] Hebrews 13:8 NKJV

[9] Throughout, "Church" refers to the Body of Christ, and "church" refers to the organized church except in direct quotes from scripture.

[10] Romans 8:19

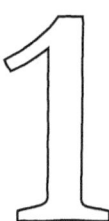

CHAPTER ONE
The Lord of the Breakthrough

> *So David went to Baal Perazim, and David defeated them there [in the valley of Rephaim] and he said, "The Lord has broken through my enemies before me, like a breakthrough of water." Therefore he called the name of that place Baal Perazim.*[1]

When the Philistines heard that David had become king of Israel[2] they assembled in the valley of Rephaim[3] to test his leadership. Concerned, David inquired of the Lord to determine what he should do. Following God's instructions, the Philistines were defeated.

David's challenge was to face a giant, but the Lord broke through on his behalf. Many of us, whether young or old, are also confronted by giant challenges during our lifetime; struggles with career, family, finances, broken relationships to name a few, but one of the greatest challenges is when our health or that of someone we care for is threatened. Whether you are battling cancer, heart disease or a life-threatening illness, remember this; God is the Lord of the breakthrough.

Micah, the prophet, declared:

> *The one who breaks open will come up before them; they will break out, pass through the gate, and go out by it; their king will pass before them, with the Lord at their head.*[4]

Micah spoke these words to the Jews of Babylon, advising them that their 70-year imprisonment was about to end. They would break out, the Lord would lead the way, and they would go back to Jerusalem through the city gate by which they had entered.

History has shown that certain individuals have been given the ability to break through insurmountable obstacles. Often unrecognized for their contribution to society until much later, these people all share one thing; they were pioneers. Jackie Robinson was one such person. In 1947, he broke the race barrier for African American baseball players. Though greatly maligned, he overcame racial hatred and widespread prejudice to open the door for thousands of players of color in Major League Baseball.[5]

A pioneer may be defined as a person who is among those who first enter or settle a region, thus opening it for occupation and development by others, or as one who is first or among the earliest in any field of inquiry, enterprise or progress.[6]

Jesus was the ultimate pioneer. He broke through the barrier of lifeless religion, making it possible for thousands to experience the life-changing realities of God.

> *Jesus was going throughout all Galilee, teaching in their synagogues and proclaiming the gospel of the kingdom, and healing every kind of disease and every kind of sickness among the people. The news about Him spread throughout all Syria; and they brought to Him all who were ill, those suffering with various diseases and pains, demoniacs, epileptics, paralytics; and He healed them. Large crowds followed Him from Galilee and the Decapolis and Jerusalem and Judea and from beyond the Jordan.*[7]

Jesus made it possible for people to experience what was considered impossible. Like a Twitter post, news that the sick were being healed went viral. Soon, thousands chased Jesus across the

Israeli countryside, hoping to experience the power of His touch. The King and His kingdom had arrived.

Where is the King today, and where is His kingdom? Across the globe there is the rising expectation that God is about to move in an unprecedented way. The thought of this is both exciting and sobering. It is exciting because grace abounds when sin abounds, and our world is in moral decay, which means a new move of God is imminent. On the other hand, this is sobering because new moves of God require new paradigm shifts on our part or we, like the Pharisees,[8] will not be able to recognize the day of God's visitation. Or worse, like the chief priests, we will plot to snuff out the move of God altogether.[9]

When the waves of revival begin to wash upon our shores we will have to boldly and courageously press forward into the new thing God is doing without fully understanding what that is. Because the majority of the Church will most likely still be functioning according to old wine skin structures,[10] we will have to don alligator skin in order to deal with the friendly fire that will erupt as we take the kingdom of heaven by force.[11]

[1] 2 Samuel 5:20 NKJV

[2] 2 Samuel 5:17-21

[3] 'Rephaim' means 'giants'

[4] Micah 2:13 NKJV

[5] http://en.wikipedia.org/wiki/Jackie_Robinson

[6] http://www.dictionary.com/browse/pioneer?s=t

[7] Matthew 4:23-25 NASB

[8] Luke 19:44

[9] Mathew 26:3-4

[10] Mark 2:22

[11] Matthew 11:12

VOLUME 6

CHAPTER TWO
The Pathway to Healing

> *But forget all that—it is nothing compared to what I am going to do. For I am about to do something new. See, I have already begun! Do you not see it? I will make a pathway through the wilderness. I will create rivers in the dry wasteland.*[1]

It was May 2016, on a **Friday afternoon,** and I had just felt something new on the back of my neck. Not familiar with this new sensation on my body I called my dear friend, Paul Cox, and asked him what I was discerning. "That's the pathway," Paul answered. "What's the pathway?" I inquired. "I'll send you the revelation I have compiled about it," he replied. I thanked him and said goodbye.

When Paul's attachment arrived, I opened it and began to read dozens of prophetic words about the pathway that had been given by different individuals, dating back to 2007. Jana Green[2] shared one of the earlier words on January 16th, 2008:

> Taste and see. Taste and see. Enlighten your senses. Practice, practice, practice; it is a new day, a new life; it is a path of Glory. It is a great hope of Glory. It is to know Him. Come let's go up to the mountain of the Lord that is

not to be touched with human hands. Come to Mount Zion. I say to Zion, "These are they to be taught on the mountain." It is a higher, holier way, a holy highway because you are called to Zion, to the New Jerusalem. Angels are gathering. There's a New Jerusalem. Call to Me, and I will answer you. There are mighty things to show you that you do not know. This is not traditional, but you are to come up higher. I want to unleash new strategies, to plunder the enemy. Dig up the fallow ground. Buried treasure, buried fruit.

On March 5th, seven weeks later, Jana received another download from the Lord:

There is the beginning of another journey and it will all come together. It is a pathway—clearing away and making a way. I want to expand My glory. Ancient path. It is a path of healing. It is a path that glows brighter to the full light of day. You must go down to go up. Deeper still. You haven't grasped what I am giving you. It is a brighter path so that the lame will not be detached, yet be healed. There are more keys and doors to be opened. It is about breakthrough. Come and see; it is about seeing. Seeing is believing; hearing is knowing; if you can have it, you can give it away. Come and see. It is a way of seeing. Breakthrough. New strategies, new weapons, new tools in the secret place, in the hiding place, I have mysteries to unfold. Come up; come up; you have gone down, now come up. It is part of the pathway. It is a higher way; it is a highway, a holy highway.

(I see doors. There are doors, different places, and gates.)

Distribution. I want to distribute. Prepare the way. Build upon this. The foundation is laid; layer upon layer of revelation is laid. What do you want to see? Ask Me.

As I read these prophetic words I wondered, "What is God trying to say and why is He revealing this to me now?" Although I didn't know the answer to either question, I suspected that God was up to something because a signs-and-wonders evangelist, Bob Koo, was scheduled to speak at our church **on Sunday morning,** two days later.

On Saturday morning I woke up and realized that I'd just had a dream. Bob Koo and I were standing across from one another as the people of Mountain View Community Church walked along a pathway in between us. Not putting two and two together yet, I recorded the dream and went on with my day. The next morning I met with Bob and Tricia Koo and our intercessory team to pray for God to move mightily during **our 10 AM** service. Twenty minutes later an intercessor, Karen Lewis, shared with the team a vision she had just had:

> I saw rows of angels making a long pathway toward the throne of God, each holding up swords that they crossed to make an archway (gate). The tips of the swords were on fire with flames and the people of God were making their way through the archway toward the throne. Emanating from the throne and running down the aisle or pathway, was a multifaceted anointing of mercy, grace, authority, healing, and new wine.

I was stunned! God had not only confirmed Jana Green's prophetic words in 2008, but also used the discernment I'd had two days earlier to shed light on Saturday's dream. The Lord's will was clear that we were to walk onto a pathway of healing in the Spirit, and then walk toward the throne of God through a gate in the heavenly realms that would lead to some kind of breakthrough. But what was the breakthrough?

Minutes later Karen Lewis began to prophesy:

> I am the way. I am bringing you into a new dimension. I have new destinies planned for each of you.

What was God up to? We were about to find out.

The spiritual climate that morning was electric as we celebrated God's presence with a heightened expectation that something big was about to happen. Bob Koo's message inspired many as he shared that if God could miraculously move through a former little boy from the jungle of Malaysia like him, He could do the same through each of us.

After Bob concluded his message, I stood up and shared what the Lord had revealed about the pathway and invited everyone to walk through it as a prophetic act. Without hesitation, the entire church lined up and slowly began to walk in front of the stage one by one. As people made their way through this heavenly roadway, it was obvious that the Lord was imparting something new and powerful.

After everyone returned to their seats, I encouraged them to pray for one another. What followed was astonishing. People in groups of two to five huddled throughout our facility and began interceding. As this unfolded, a member of our church, Kevin Wada, brought forward a father, mother and their nine-year old daughter. I learned later that Kevin had invited them to our service so the girl could receive prayer for a rare form of leukemia that she had contracted two years earlier. This type of leukemia was so rare that the little girl's doctors were unsure how to treat her and had recently informed her parents that the next round of chemo could possibly take her life. Poked, pricked and cut for two years this nine-year-old no longer wanted to live. Hope had waned, and the stage was now set for the Lord to move.

Kevin, Tricia Koo, and another church member named Diana Stewart laid hands on the girl and asked the Lord to heal her. Diana shared later that while praying she smelled a foul odor (the spirit of cancer?) leaving the girl, and the mom smelled it too.

The next day the little girl was scheduled for a routine blood test. When the blood count results came back it read ANC 1606, WBC 2.2, HGB 10.7, and platelets 171, meaning that she was healthy enough to leave the hospital. That night her parents posted on Facebook the hash tag, #miracles in the air, and joyously announced that their daughter no longer had leukemia. Barely able to contain my excitement, I posted on Facebook a snapshot of Kevin, Tricia and Diana praying for the girl along with a brief caption about what happened. Within 72 hours, the news of this amazing miracle went viral as 3,355 people viewed the post. Just as exciting was the news that the family Kevin had invited to church are Mormons.[3]

Back to the rest of the story—at the same time the little girl was receiving prayer, others in the congregation were also being prayed for regarding a variety of physical conditions. Days later, the testimonies began rolling in:

> Lisa reported that after her son prayed for her, her migraine headaches lifted (and have not returned since).
>
> Joni posted on Facebook that after three others prayed for her she was asthma free.
>
> Donna confirmed that her neck had been healed.
>
> Our associate pastor, Jason Lehfeldt, reported that his knee was healed after receiving prayer from a young man named Ryley. In turn, he had prayed for Ryley's injured knee and it was healed too.
>
> Another woman named Lisa confirmed that she was healed of severe sciatic pain that was shooting down her leg and as well as a three-week-long nagging cough.
>
> Richard reported that he was instantly healed of a painful hand condition and pain in his legs.
>
> A young mother of three, Bobbie, who was deaf in one ear shared over the phone that she was partially healed and has started to hear muffled sounds in the affected ear.

Several days later I began to wonder if this healing outbreak was just a one-time occurrence or something new the Lord was birthing. Shortly after that, I received an encouraging email from

Paul Cox, who forwarded a scripture that his son, Brian, had sent to him:

> *Trust in the Lord with all your heart, and lean not on your own understanding; In all your ways acknowledge Him, and He shall direct your paths. Do not be wise in your own eyes; Fear the Lord and depart from evil. It will be health to your flesh, and strength to your bones.*[4]

Reading this, I was encouraged to know that there was at least one verse in Scripture that confirmed that there is a pathway that is intertwined with physical healing. Curious, I searched in the Bible to see if there were any other verses relevant to pathways and physical healing, and confirmed further that we were on the right path (pun intended):

> *Therefore strengthen the hands which hang down, and the feeble knees, and make straight paths for your feet, so that what is lame may not be dislocated, but rather be healed.*[5]

Now I felt even better, but asked, "Is the pathway limited only to physical healing of the body?" To my pleasant surprise, I came across two verses that answered my question:

> *He restores my soul; He leads me in the paths of righteousness for His name's sake.*[6]

> *Thus says the Lord: "Stand in the ways and see, and ask for the old paths, where the good way is, and walk in it; then you will find rest for your souls."*[7]

After reading theses verses about the pathway and their reference to both physical healing of the body and inner healing of the soul, I was 98% convinced that the Lord was doing something new. Two percent of me still wondered however, if the healing outbreak we had experienced the previous Sunday would continue the following weekend. There's an old saying, "The proof is in the pudding." I needed more evidence.

A week later, a man from California visited our church. After the service he shared that two women had prayed for his knee and wrist, and he had experienced healing. He had also requested prayer from the two ladies for a slipped disc in his lower back but that had not been healed yet. I could see that he really wanted to be well, so I asked if I could pray for him and he gladly agreed. As I laid my hand on the injured area I heard the Holy Spirit whisper, "Speak to the disc and tell it to shift." Out of obedience, I quietly whispered, "Shift!" Within seconds, the Holy Spirit began to do something, and I felt the man trembling in the Lord's presence; and within minutes he began to tear up as he felt the Lord shifting his disc into place. Then, in a God-inspired moment, he turned to his wife and daughter and hugged them tightly as tears ran down his face. It truly was a privilege for me to witness the Lord's performance of this miracle on behalf of His precious son and his family. Four days later, his sister-in-law confirmed that the Lord had indeed healed her brother-in-law's back, and his older brother reported that the man's daughter was so greatly impacted by her father's healing that several days later she led her eighty-year-old grandmother to Jesus.

In retrospect, not only did the Lord shift this man's disc into proper alignment, but He also confirmed that He had shifted the people of Mountain View into a new dimension of His healing power. The Bible says that God is continually transforming us from glory to glory into the image of His Son.[8] I believe this transformation includes not only Christ's character and His mission, but also His ministry of healing the sick and setting captives free.

As I reflect on all of this, I realize that in the natural a path or pathway is a trail, route or road that has been paved or carved by others who have preceded them.[9] Once we walk or drive onto a pathway, it presumably leads us to a specific destination. In the Bible, a path or pathway is symbolic of our journey to the Father,[10] which is why our relationship with Jesus is referred to as a walk.[11] God does not, however, control or manipulate our walk with Him, but extends an ongoing invitation to bless us if we faithfully follow Him along His paths in both the natural and heavenly realms. We can, of course, choose to stay on or to depart from the pathway; but we should know that the first choice results in physical healing, spiritual renewal and divine protection.[12]

Based on what transpired on May 15th, 2016, and considering the four Bible verses cited earlier,[13] it is my belief that God in eternity past created a heavenly pathway that imparts healing gifts to the Body of Christ, enabling us to supernaturally impact people's lives. For years I have wondered if Jesus' words would ever come to pass that God's people, not just five-fold officers,[14] would lay their hands on the sick and see them recover:

> *And these signs will accompany those who believe: in my name they will cast out demons; they will speak in new tongues; they will pick up serpents with their hands; and if they drink any deadly poison, it will not hurt them; they will lay their hands on the sick, and they will recover." So then the Lord Jesus, after he had spoken to them, was taken up into heaven and sat down at the right hand of God. And they went out and preached everywhere, while the Lord worked with them and confirmed the message by accompanying signs.*[15]

Now, it has happened!

---

[1] Isaiah 43:18-19 NLT

[2] Jana Green is an artist, prayer minister and prophetic intercessor. Her website is http://www.signsandwondersstudio.com

[3] Kevin intends to invite this family back to church in the near future to give them the opportunity to publicly thank Jesus for performing this incredible miracle for their daughter. He has also been helping them raise money to help pay off the medical expenses related to their daughter's two-year battle with cancer.

[4] Proverbs 3:5-8 NKJV

[5] Hebrews 12:12-13 NKJV

[6] Psalm 23:3 NKJV

[7] Jeremiah 6:16 NKJV

[8] 1 Corinthians 3:18

[9] http://Strongs Concordance/Path, (Derekh, #1870)
[10] John 14:6
[11] Galatians 5:16
[12] Isaiah 35:5-10
[13] Proverbs 3:5-8, Hebrews 12:12-13, Psalm 23:3, Jeremiah 6:16
[14] Ephesians 4:11-13
[15] Mark 16:17-20

CHAPTER THREE

I Want My Church Back!

> *Remember not the former things, nor consider the things of old. Behold, I am doing a new thing; now it springs forth, do you not perceive it? I will make a way in the wilderness and rivers in the desert.*[1]

On May 9th, 2016, the Elijah List posted, *In the Next Five Months, We Will Be Under the Grip of a Revolutionary Wind of Reformation*, by Johnny Enlow, author of the Seven Mountain Prophecy, who wrote:

> For lack of expanded language, we are crying out and sensing revival, but what is needed and what is coming is revolutionary reformation. 85% of American Christians are not regular churchgoers. Over 95% of churchgoers don't tithe because they are not convinced it is biblical. 75% of the pastors of these churches regularly think of quitting and struggle with depression. Fifteen thousand pastors actually do quit or are fired every year, usually over a moral issue.

Without judging either side, this all goes to establish that church and Christians need more than revival. We can call it revival, but what we need is an overhauling reformation. We are not close to what church needs to look like, so reviving what we have is not enough.

Furthermore, perhaps only 1% of churches even attempt their biblical assignment of "equipping the saints for the work of the ministry" (Ephesians 4:11-13). And then, maybe only 1% of that 1% actually equip the saints for anything other than church ministry. The saints are to be equipped for their 9-to-5 assignments, and that only begins to happen as one embraces some version of the seven-mountain mandate.

If you are shocked at my assessment of church and church life, it is actually much worse than what I have so far stated. I believe that 95% of churches don't even have a grid for the kingdom of God and how it is coming. Additionally, it is still more the exception than the rule that the Holy Spirit is given any priority in church settings. The Church is also perhaps 100 years behind even society's light as to properly emancipating and empowering women. Sunday mornings are still the most racist and the most sexist hour in America. Find the list of the top 100 churches of America, and you will find, almost without exception, something very ritualized, male-dominated, and male-driven.

So, how are we going to go from an assembly-line model, Holy-Spirit deprived, non-equipping, personal kingdom building church that is burning out both pastors and members, to a living, loving, relational, Holy Spirit-presence filled, societally-engaged Church? Only major help from above is going to get us there—and that is what is coming. That help is going to look like a bulldozer. The Holy Spirit will fall on and ignite the new, but it will also come in and clear out spaces for the new. Most of us are

> not even in a good enough place to sort out how this will all happen.
>
> Blaming pastors is not the answer, though it is the easiest thing to do. I was a senior pastor myself for 14 years, and I can tell you that at least 20% of members are toxic members who go around from church to church leaving the debris of their own woundedness. We are going to begin to experience the extreme makeover of the church of Jesus Christ, and we ALL need to repent and make adjustments. We need new models of doing church, but then, most of all, a greater embracement of love and forgiveness. This is a specific job for the Holy Spirit, and He will be up for the task. He is going to pour His liquid, fiery love over us all, and it will be amazing what levels of unity, love, and humility that we will embrace that will allow us to begin to experience the profound changes that are coming. We will soon be doing more good than harm![2]

Johnny Enlow's statement above is hard to swallow but if we are honest we must agree, at least partially, that his assessment of the present-day Church is true. Without God's intervention we will continue to be frustrated and fruitless. Change is coming.

In 1997, a disturbing dream found me standing on a 200-foot-high wall, within walking distance of Ala Moana Beach on Oahu's southern shore. Looking out toward the horizon, I saw my wife and children standing to my right, but was horrified to see an enormous 900-foot wave rushing toward us at MACH speed. As this monstrous wave sped towards us, a large hand pulled and placed me somewhere off to the side, where I watched helplessly as the wave encompassed the entire wall. The scene slowed down and I saw hundreds of believers standing across the top of the wall as far as my eye could see, but as the wave washed over the wall it swept all of the believers down to their deaths. Then to my utter dismay, my wife, Barbara, was swept down to her death too. In the final scene I woke up crying, "My bride is dead! My bride is dead!"

Time and again, I have reflected about this and asked, "God, what is this dream about?" Over the years some have shared their belief that an actual tidal wave will strike Hawaii in the future, but I don't believe this is what God was saying. Here's my take:

> The number 2 symbolizes the word witness or testimony. When multiplied by 100 (the 200 foot wall), God was saying, "This is really important, listen carefully, I am testifying what is going to transpire."
>
> The wall represented or symbolized a watchtower,[3] while my standing off to the side of the wall was symbolic of a watchman being set apart.[4]
>
> The number 9 represented either the fruit of the Spirit,[5] the gifts of the Spirit,[6] the hour of prayer,[7] or finality (Jesus **died at 3 pm** or at the 9th hour).[8]
>
> With 9 multiplied by 100, and given the context of the dream, it seems that the number 9 symbolized God's urgent call for church-wide intercession for the transformational changes that God would be orchestrating in the Hawaiian islands in the years to come. The believers and my wife (representing the Bride of Christ) who fell to their deaths symbolized the Church in Hawaii and its present day structures or wineskins that would be brought to death in order to come into sync with the kingdom of God and His plans for Hawaii.

Several months after having this dramatic dream, I attended an all-night intercessory gathering of five thousand people at the Kemper Arena in Kansas City, The Watch of the Lord®. At 3 AM Mahesh Chavda, the leader of the gathering, said that God was calling certain individuals in the arena to stand on the wall and watch for the Lord. Seconds later, the Spirit of the Lord came upon me and I began to shake violently. Recognizing what the Lord was declaring, my friend, Dean Fujishima, pointed at me and said, "Rob! Remember your dream. You were standing on a wall. God is calling you to be a watchmen on the wall!"

EXPLORING HEAVENLY PLACES

In 1997, I launched a chapter of the Watch of the Lord® in Hawaii. For five years, intercessors from over twenty churches gathered on a monthly basis to pray for the Lord to unite the Church in Hawaii and birth revival.

Toward the end of 1996, several months before the dream, a large group of pastors gathered at First Assembly of God Red Hill on a stormy Friday evening. A pastor I had just met walked up to me and said, "Rob, God wants you to step out by faith tonight." As a Southern Baptist I responded, "What does that mean?" "Just trust Him and step out by faith," he replied, and then laid hands on me. I crumpled to the floor as the power of God rippled through my entire body. Within moments my stomach began to quiver up and down as if air was being pumped into my body. As this was happening another pastor stooped down beside me and whispered, "Rob, the Lord wants you to prophesy." I asked, "What's that?" "Speak out what the Lord is saying to your spirit." "Great" I thought, "What does that mean?" Seconds later, the presence of the Lord intensified inside of me and I began to declare at the top of my lungs that the wind of God's Spirit, a great awakening, would blow through the Hawaiian Islands, sweeping tens of thousands into the kingdom of God. As I decreed God's heart for Hawaii, I was filled with emotions that I cannot describe. Minutes later, the Holy Spirit welled up inside of me again like water about to burst out of a dam and I began to weep profusely, crying out, "I want My Church back! I want My Church back!"

Engulfed by God's fiery presence for the next half hour I was changed forever as I experienced the revelation that the Father is Power.[9, 10] I also knew during this supernatural encounter that God was going to bring to pass, without any doubt, what He had just declared. Still, as a Southern Baptist I wondered if my experience could be verified somewhere in the Bible. After a lengthy search, two verses brought peace to my heart:

> *But on the way to Naioth in Ramah the Spirit of God came even upon Saul, and he, too, began to prophesy all the way to Naioth! He tore off his clothes and lay naked on the ground all day and all*

night, prophesying in the presence of Samuel. The people who were watching exclaimed, "What? Is even Saul a prophet?" [11]

[1] Isaiah 43:18-19 ESV

[2] http://www.elijahlist.com/words/display_word.html?ID=16046

[3] Isaiah 21:6-8

[4] Ezekiel 33:1-9

[5] Galatians 5:22

[6] 1 Corinthians 12:4-11

[7] Acts 3:1, 10:30

[8] Mark 15:25

[9] Matthew 26:64

[10] Power of God is covered extensively in Volumes 4 and 5 of the *Exploring Heavenly Places* Series.

[11] 1 Samuel 19:23-24

CHAPTER FOUR
Revival, Revolution, Reformation

For the past decade Barbara and I have gone weekly to have our spines adjusted by a chiropractor. Chiropractors do more than 'crack your back'; they align your vertebrae so your entire body is able to experience unhindered nerve flow. Every time our chiropractor finishes adjusting us he says, "The power is on!" Even though I initially thought this post adjustment mantra was odd, I understood that he was simply saying, "Now that your vertebrae are properly aligned your central nervous system can function at maximum capacity." I believe that we, the New Testament Church, have yet to function at our maximum capacity because we have not been aware of the power that is available to us to help others, and we have not correctly aligned ourselves with the Holy Spirit.

In the fall of 1996, I attended the annual Hawaii Baptist Convention at a seaside hotel on Maui. During the opening meeting the electricity inexplicably went off. As we sat in the dark waiting for hotel personnel to restore power to the building the Lord whispered to me, "My Church is powerless!"

When it became clear that power would not be restored that evening, the session was cancelled and we returned to our rooms to sleep. Still unable to restore power the next day, the conference was cancelled and I returned to Oahu.

The early Church operated at a level of spiritual power that transformed their world. Tragically, many people believe today that when the first century apostles died the power that undergirded their ministry ceased with them. If the power of the Holy Spirit left the Church, then why does Hebrews 13:8 say that Jesus is the same today, yesterday and forever? And even more importantly, if the power of God is not available to us to help those suffering from a wide range of spiritual, emotional and physical issues, then what is our game plan for helping them?

If we are going to see the present day Church return to the same level of fruitfulness that the early Church experienced, we have no choice but to invite the Holy Spirit back into our midst. To effect this shift, the Lord has been steadily restoring the offices of apostle and prophet to the Church over the last three decades to train and equip His people to move in kingdom power.[1]

In 1998, I had a startling dream in which I was lying facedown in a mountainside ditch. In the distance I heard the sound of thunderous footsteps approaching. Looking up, I saw three giant tyrannosaurs marching toward me. As these giant lizards passed in front of me, I felt the ground shake and heard the Lord declare, "I am restoring apostles to My Church!"

The first century apostles perpetuated the kingdom of God via powerful signs and wonders.[2] They healed the sick, set captives free and proclaimed the Gospel of the kingdom everywhere they went.[3] They were church-planting trailblazers who established kingdom culture wherever they proclaimed the Gospel.

In 1992, my wife and I planted Mountain View Community Church. We were trained and equipped to start a seeker-sensitive, purpose-driven church, and this is what we set out to do. Our Sunday service consisted of twenty minutes of worship, a few announcements, a five-minute dramatic presentation and a short how-to message. Many gave their lives to Christ, and the church grew. The ongoing challenge we faced, however, was that we weren't able to help those the Lord had sent us to break free from issues such as anger, depression, fear and lust. The truth was that we were only able to pull off our weekly service, leaving no room for God to heal the sick, break off spiritual bondages or prophetically encourage the faint hearted.

The 'kahal', or 'assembly of God' in the wilderness [4] was not a program-driven congregation but a presence-led Body. They followed the cloud by day and the fire of God's presence by night.[5] If the cloud remained stationary, they camped and rested. If the cloud moved, they moved. They never considered asking the cloud to follow them; they followed the cloud.

During His brief, three-year ministry, Jesus healed the sick and set captives free. He will do the same today if we invite Him to do so. In a brief, early-morning dream the Lord spoke to me and said, "Rob, don't debate, demonstrate!" Telling people they are going to hell doesn't usher them into the kingdom, but neither do how-to messages that don't release the life-changing power of the Holy Spirit. We are not called to debate people into the kingdom of God. We are called to reveal the King and His kingdom through supernatural demonstrations of His love.

In the fall of 1987, I enrolled at Golden Gate Seminary in Marin County California. During the first semester I was invited to join a team of people who wanted to share the gospel on the campus of UC Berkley, which has a diverse student population that is not easy to engage. Arriving on campus, our group leader decided to set up shop at one of the campus entrances. With a bull horn in hand he stood on a box and started to yell, "Turn or burn! Turn or burn!" Not expecting him to do this and feeling extremely embarrassed I retreated quickly to the sideline. Not surprisingly, an angry crowd gathered to challenge what he was saying, shouting back expletives as he continued to tell them where they would end up if they did not repent.

My heart is not to condemn the man who engaged the students of UC Berkley that day, as I believe he genuinely wanted to see people receive Jesus as their personal Lord and Savior. His motive was pure, but his method was poor.

What was Jesus' method of engaging pre-believers? The apostle Paul said:

> *I came to you in weakness—timid and trembling. And my message and my preaching were very plain. Rather than using clever and persuasive speeches, I relied only on the power of the Holy Spirit. I did this so you would trust not in human wisdom but in the power of God.*[6]

What is the power that Paul referred to? And is that power available to us today to reach those who don't know Jesus, and help those who do? Jesus stated that signs or demonstrations of power would accompany us:

> *These miraculous signs will accompany those who believe: They will cast out demons in my name, and they will speak in new languages. They will be able to handle snakes with safety, and if they drink anything poisonous, it won't hurt them. They will be able to place their hands on the sick, and they will be healed.*[7]

These verses beg the following questions:
- Are supernatural signs following us?
- Are we making room for God to move as He wills?
- What are we afraid will happen if we give control of the Church back to God?

Are supernatural signs following us? Acts 3:1-11 is an awe-inspiring story about a crippled man whose ability to walk was instantly restored by two of Jesus' followers:

> *Peter and John went to the Temple one afternoon to take part in the three o'clock prayer service. As they approached the Temple, a man lame from birth was being carried in. Each day he was put beside the Temple gate, the one called the Beautiful Gate, so he could beg from the people going into the Temple. When he saw Peter and John about to enter, he asked them for some money. Peter and John*

> *looked at him intently, and Peter said, "Look at us!" The lame man looked at them eagerly, expecting some money. But Peter said, "I don't have any silver or gold for you. But I'll give you what I have. In the name of Jesus Christ the Nazarene, get up and walk!" Then Peter took the lame man by the right hand and helped him up. And as he did, the man's feet and ankles were instantly healed and strengthened. He jumped up, stood on his feet, and began to walk! Then, walking, leaping, and praising God, he went into the Temple with them. All the people saw him walking and heard him praising God. When they realized he was the lame beggar they had seen so often at the Beautiful Gate, they were absolutely astounded! They all rushed out in amazement to Solomon's Colonnade, where the man was holding tightly to Peter and John.*

What I find even more fascinating than this miraculous healing is that miracles of this kind were the norm, not the exception, throughout the Book of Acts. If Jesus is the same today as He was yesterday, then why aren't we seeing the same manifestations of His power now? The lack of power in the Church today is baffling. Everywhere Jesus went He wreaked havoc on the kingdom of darkness:

> *And you know that God anointed Jesus of Nazareth with the Holy Spirit and with power. Then Jesus went around doing good and healing all who were oppressed by the devil, for God was with him.*[8]

Today, the kingdom of darkness is spreading throughout our nation at an alarming rate. Saddled with trillions of dollars of debt and facing the reality of global terror, regular natural disasters, widespread political discord and broken families, we are teetering on the precipice of a national meltdown. In spite of this, the average churchgoer is oblivious to the works of the evil one, who is systematically destroying our families through absentee parenting, alcoholism, divorce, drugs, and sexual abuse.

The coordinated attack by Osama Bin Laden's henchmen on September 9, 2011, was a wake up call for the Church to arise but instead, we rolled over, pushed the snooze button and went right back to sleep. 9/11 was not just a terrorist attack; it was a deadly object lesson of how a few dedicated men, albeit on the wrong side of righteousness, can change the course of a nation if they are willing to sacrifice their lives for a cause they believe in.

Jesus recruited, trained and empowered twelve men to sacrifice their lives for the gospel. Because they boldly declared the gospel with signs following they changed the destiny of their own generation and all generations to follow. They first went to the religious structures of their day, the synagogues and the temple, but when they were not received they took the Gospel into the marketplace. Everywhere they went, they healed the sick, set captives free and led people to Jesus. We can do the same if we are willing to lay down our agendas in favor of the agenda of the Holy Spirit.

[1] Ephesians 4:11-13, 2 Corinthians 12:12

[2] Acts 4:29-30,5:12-16

[3] Acts 1:8, 8:5-7; Romans 15:16-19; 2 Corinthians 12:12

[4] Acts 7:38

[5] Exodus 13:21

[6] 1 Corinthians 2:3-5 NLT

[7] Mark 16:17-18 NLT

[8] Acts 10:38 NLT

CHAPTER FIVE

From Orphans to Sons and Daughters

No, I will not abandon you as orphans—I will come to you.[1]

Yet you brought me safely from my mother's womb and led me to trust you at my mother's breast.[2]

One of the primary challenges the Church faces today is our dependence on formulas, or planned, air-tight programs, instead of seeking the breast, or intimate revelatory leading, of El Shaddai. El Shaddai[3] means, 'God is my breast'. How are we going to experience genuine revival if we don't wean ourselves off of human formula? In order to break free from our agendas and follow the Father's agenda, we must allow the Holy Spirit to transform us from orphans into sons and daughters. In John 5:19, Jesus revealed that sonship was and is the key to kingdom success:

> *I tell you the truth, the Son can do nothing by himself. He does only what he sees the Father doing. Whatever the Father does, the Son also does.*

The Son was in sync with the Father at all times, sharing an intimate bond that could not be broken. In the Garden of Gethsemane, Jesus pleaded with the Father to let the cup of His impending suffering pass from Him,[4] not because He feared the physical pain and torture of crucifixion but because He feared being severed from His Father's love for the first time.[5] The thought of being separated from His Father frightened Jesus, the Son, so much that He momentarily thought of bypassing the cross. But instead of succumbing to what must have been overwhelming fear, Jesus pressed forward for the joy set before Him.[6] What was this joy? It was the joy of knowing that if He allowed Himself to be separated from His Father on the cross, He would make it possible for wayward orphans to know the Father intimately in the same way He did.

At a pivotal moment in human history, the Son, became estranged from the Father when He cried out, "My God, My God, why have you forsaken me?"[7] That is, He experienced for the first time what it meant to be separated from the Father's love, literally becoming an orphan, thus making it possible for us, as orphans, to become sons and daughters. At the cross, Jesus not only removed the sin that separated us from the Father, but He also made it possible for us to return to our original design and begin to function accordingly.

In Luke 3:38, Adam is referred to as a son of God. In the garden, Adam was a son, not an orphan. He enjoyed the pleasure of knowing God intimately and was endued with supernatural strength, intelligence and eternal life. At the Fall, Adam lost his original identity as God's son when he and Eve ate from the tree of the knowledge of good and evil.[8] From that point forward, Adam functioned no longer as a son but as an orphan. Instead of walking intimately with the Father, he feared Him and was ashamed of his own inadequacies.[9]

As mentioned above, when Jesus died on the cross He made it possible for us to be restored to our original design. He came as the Second Adam to restore our true identity and our heavenly DNA that was stolen at Eden:

> *Thus it is written, "The first man Adam became a living being"; the last Adam became a life-giving spirit. But it is not the spiritual that*

> *is first but the natural, and then the spiritual. The first man was from the earth, a man of dust; the second man is from heaven. As was the man of dust, so also are those who are of the dust, and as is the man of heaven, so also are those who are of heaven. Just as we have borne the image of the man of dust, we shall also bear the image of the man of heaven.*[10]

If we, the sons and daughters of God, are to be revealed to all of creation,[11] we must ask the Son of God to remove every false image that masks our true identity as the revealed sons of God. When this occurs, we will be supernaturally transitioned back to our original design, causing us to rely less and less upon human formula and more and more upon the leading of the many-breasted One. In effect, the transformation from orphans into mature sons and daughters will enable us to discern good from evil[12] and to know what the Father is doing. Once we know what the Father is doing, we will begin to perform the greater works that Jesus prophesied.[13]

One of my favorite martial arts actors of all time was Bruce Lee. Whether he fought in Kung Fu tournaments, or acted on the big movie screen, everyone knew that Lee was able to defeat anyone, anytime, anywhere. Lee attributed his success to a style of martial arts called Jeet Kune Do. In the screenplay of the 1973, Warner Brothers film, *Enter the Dragon*, Lee was asked, "What's your style?" He replied, "My style? You can call it the art of fighting without fighting." [14]

Jeet Kune Do was a form of Chinese Kung Fu without form. Through his studies Lee came to believe that styles had become too rigid and unrealistic. He called martial art competitions of the day dry land swimming, and believed real combat was spontaneous, and that a martial artist could not predict, but only react; and a good martial artist should be like water, moving fluidly without hesitation.[15]

Although I do not believe in or in any way support the Yin Yang philosophy that undergirds Jeet Kune Do, I do believe that the Church can learn from Lee's example and become far more fluid as led by the Holy Spirit, and far less formula driven by human agendas. This doesn't mean that we shouldn't plan or minimize excellence in order to move in the Spirit, but it does mean that as sons and daughters we will only do what we see our Papa doing. This will seem risky for many, but others will take the plunge and discover the joy of only doing what they see their heavenly Father doing.

To defeat each opponent, Bruce Lee strategically selected the specific style of Kung Fu that would most effectively combat his or her particular fighting style. In the spiritual realm, the devil cannot be defeated if we aren't aware of what he is doing.[16] This awareness is referred to in Hebrews 5:14 as discernment. I will share much more about this very necessary spiritual gift as we proceed.

During the Persian Gulf War in 1980, Saddam Hussein launched forty-two Scud missiles [17] at Israel, of which thirty-eight actually landed within Israel's borders, killing two people and destroying thousands of homes and apartments. The loss of life was awful, yet the casualties could have been substantially higher if Hussein would have had better missile technology at his disposal.

While Hussein was launching Scud missiles at cities throughout Israel, U.S. forces were launching laser-guided missiles, or smart bombs, to pummel strategic military targets throughout Iraq. Unlike the Scuds that were fired in the general direction towards populated areas in hope of killing Israelis, the laser-guided missiles hit specific targets with pinpoint accuracy, minimizing collateral damage.

We are in a war for our families and our nation(s), and it seems at times that the enemy is winning. We cannot afford to battle evil with Scud-missile prayers that are launched toward the kingdom of darkness, hoping to turn the tide. Instead, the Father wants us to wage war with the enemy as sons and daughters who are able discern what He is doing,[18] and respond strategically by launching laser-guided prayers and declarations that destroy the works of the enemy with pinpoint accuracy. Next, I will share how the gift of discernment has made it supernaturally possible to heal the sick and set captives free in both the Church and marketplace.

[1] John 14:18 NLT
[2] Psalm 22:9 NLT
[3] Jewish Studies Blog by Dr. Eli, http://www.jewishstudies.eteacher.com
[4] Matthew 26:39
[5] Mark 15:34
[6] Hebrews 12:2
[7] Mark 15:33-34
[8] Genesis 3:6-7
[9] Genesis 3:8-10
[10] 1 Corinthians 15:45-49 ESV
[11] Romans 8:19
[12] Hebrews 5:14
[13] John 14:12
[14] https://en.wikipedia.org/wiki/Bruce_Lee
[15] Ibid.
[16] 2 Corinthians 2:11-12
[17] https://en.wikipedia.org/wiki/Gulf_War
[18] John 5:19

VOLUME 6

CHAPTER SIX
Miracles on the Mountain of the Lord

> Yet I dare not boast about anything except what Christ has done through me, bringing the Gentiles to God by my message and by the way I worked among them. They were convinced by the power of miraculous signs and wonders and by the power of God's Spirit. In this way, I have fully presented the Good News of Christ from Jerusalem all the way to Illyricum.[1]

When I was a kid, one of my favorite places to eat ice cream was Baskin-Robins. Their catchy marketing phrase was, "What's your flavor? 31 to choose from." Like Baskin-Robbins' 31 flavors of ice cream, *Miracles On the Mountain of the Lord* features 31 different categories of miracles the Lord has performed over the last twenty years in and through the people of Mountain View Community Church, each of which has been unique. The Lord's desire is to express His creative genius through us, the Church:

> God's purpose in all this was to use the church to display His wisdom in its rich variety to all the unseen rulers and authorities in the heavenly places. This was his eternal plan, which he carried out through Christ Jesus our Lord.[2]

By definition, miracles are instantaneous, while healing typically takes place over time. Whether immediate or gradual, God loves to reveal Himself as Healer because He truly loves and cares about us. May the following accounts of the miraculous hand of God open your eyes to the realm of the supernatural, and encourage you to believe that all things are possible with God.

Miscellaneous Signs and Wonders (Category 1)

> *Now Stephen, a man full of God's grace and power, performed great wonders and signs among the people.*[3]

After ringing the doorbell, I waited for my friend, Fili, to emerge.

"Rob, what are you doing here?" he asked with a puzzled look on his face.

"You invited me, Fili!"

"No, I didn't, he replied."

"Yes, you did," I insisted.

After giving it some thought, Fili figured out that he had accidentally invited me to his home, confusing my last name in his Rolodex with one of his leaders who had a similar name. Nevertheless, I am very thankful that he did ask me into his home that evening to hear his friends, Gord and Jan Whyte, share their remarkable testimony about the power of God's love.

Jan had arrived in a village of a third-world nation dressed in a brand new, sparkling-white, three-piece pants suit. Walking into the village, she spotted a woman caked in mud from head to toe. The Holy Spirit whispered, "Jan, go over to that woman and give her a big hug on My behalf." "But Lord," she argued, "I'd love to hug her, but my brand new clothes will get dirty." God persisted, "Jan, love on her for Me."

She protested a second time, explaining to the Lord that although she wanted to do as He asked, it wasn't possible because her new suit would be ruined. Un-persuaded, the Lord said a third time, "Jan, I want you to hug her," and sensing His heart for this woman, Jan finally relented.

With an interpreter at her side, Jan approached the woman and asked for permission to give her a hug. The woman agreed, and Jan hugged her tightly. A few moments later, the woman began to jump up and down, squealing with joy. "Ask her what's going on," Jan said to the interpreter, who then reported, "She just said she was blind but now she can see."

If you feel called to pray for the sick, remember this: It is God's unquenchable love that heals! It's not about performing great exploits for God. It's simple. It's about loving on people on behalf of the Lord. There is nothing more powerful.

As I was saying goodbye to members of our church family on a Sunday afternoon, Phil came up and requested prayer for the back of his knee. I obliged, and waited for the Holy Spirit to show up. A minute later, Phil bent his knees together and began to sway side to side as if he was skiing down a mountain slope. As this was happening, he shared that he felt like he was swiveling back and forth on ball bearings. Needless to say, Phil left the parking lot that day with no pain behind his right knee.

A mother and her newly converted son attended a newcomers' meeting at our church office. Skeptical of his newfound passion for God and the church, she had come to check us out. As the meeting drew to a close, I shared that the Lord wanted to heal someone with a bad back and we began praying for one another. Five minutes later I noticed this mother swiveling her hips back and forth in a circular motion like she had a hula-hoop around her waist. This odd manifestation lasted for fifteen minutes. "What are you doing Lord?" I wondered.

Later, the woman who prayed for her reported with great excitement, "She said that she has had chronic lower back pain for twenty-five years, and every time her hips rotated back and forth the pain in her back gradually decreased, until it was completely gone! The Lord has healed her!"

There is no one kinder than Jesus. Instead of condemning this woman for her doubt and unbelief, He healed her back! Eventually she received the Lord, got baptized and became a faithful member of our church. Hallelujah!

Martha, a retired woman in our congregation, requested prayer for her ailing back. I asked the Lord to meet her request and the presence of God came upon her immediately. Right before my eyes and with her husband standing at her side, Martha began to bend backwards like she was doing the limbo. Unbelievably, the back of her head nearly touched the floor, which was amazing because she was in her mid-sixties. In the natural, Martha could never have bent backwards, yet she did. Several minutes later, the Lord's presence lifted and she stood tall and said, "My back is healed!"

After a Sunday service, four retired ladies visiting our church requested prayer. Interestingly, all four had neck issues. As I was about to pray, I smelled frankincense and myrrh in the Spirit. When this happens it appears that the Lord is about to release His healing power.

> *All thy [God's] garments smell of frankincense and myrrh, and aloes, and cassia, out of the ivory palaces, whereby they have made thee glad.*[4]

To my astonishment, all four ladies reported that God had healed their necks. There was no prayer, no laying on of hands, nothing. God revealed what He was about to do with the discernment of smell, and then He sovereignly did it.

[1] Romans 15:18-19 NLT
[2] Ephesians 3:10 NLT

[3] Acts 6:8 NIV
[4] Psalm 45:8 KJV

CHAPTER SEVEN
Anxiety, Fear and Stress *(Category 2)*

> *While Israel was staying in Shittim, the men began to indulge in sexual immorality with Moabite women, who invited them to the sacrifices to their gods. The people ate the sacrificial meal and bowed down before these gods. So Israel yoked themselves to the Baal of Peor. And the Lord's anger burned against them.*[1]

The phone rang. On the other end was one of our ministry team leaders. Crying, she said, "I don't know what's going on. I am stressed out and filled with **overwhelming fear and anxiety**." A few questions later it was apparent that there was no rational reason for her anxiety, and I was stumped. Moments later, I felt a painful sensation between my navel and my pubic bone. I'm going to ask you a difficult question, "Have you ever had an abortion?" "No, I haven't, but I have had a miscarriage," she replied.

Hosea 9:11-14[2] is a passage that may explain why so many women have miscarriages:

> *Ephraim's glory shall fly away like a bird—no birth, no pregnancy, no conception! Even if they bring up children, I will bereave them till is left. Woe to them when I depart from them! Ephraim, as I have seen, was like a young palm planted in a meadow; but Ephraim*

must lead his children out to slaughter. Give them, O Lord—what will you give? Give them a miscarrying womb and dry breasts.

Could this woman's fear and anxiousness be connected to the worship of Molech? Molech was the fire god of the Canaanite people who engaged in the vile practice of sacrificing innocent children in exchange for Molech's favor-a good crop, protection from one's enemies, etc.

I asked if she was willing to repent of Molech worship on behalf of her family generational line, explaining that such child sacrifice was equivalent to abortion and suggesting the possibility that her anxiety might be connected to such worship. Desperate for relief, she repented of this possible iniquity, and to her amazement the anxiety immediately lifted. Hanging up the phone, I wondered if the evil one has a legal right to cause miscarriages because of ancestral worship of Molech.

The March of Dimes reports that as many as 50% of all pregnancies end in miscarriage, most often before a woman misses a menstrual period or even knows she is pregnant. About 15-25% of recognized pregnancies also end in miscarriage, and more than 80% of miscarriages occur within the first three months of pregnancy.[3]

According to the medical community, the possible causes of miscarriages include diabetes, hormonal problems, infection, thyroid issues, and uterine abnormalities.[4] Mental health research has shown that women who have had a miscarriage often suffer from anxiety, with up to 1 in 5 experiencing anxiety levels similar to people attending psychiatric outpatient services, and up to one-third of them are clinically depressed.[5]

Is it possible that we have stumbled upon a biblical solution for the anxiety women deal with post-miscarriage? A solution that may well be as simple as a prayer of restitution[6] that repents for and renounces the sacrifice of innocent children in the generational line.

[1] Numbers 25:1-3
[2] ESV
[3] http://www.webmd.com/baby/guide/pregnancy-miscarriage#1
[4] *What Causes Miscarriages?* http://www.en.webmd/
[5] *Miscarriage and Ectopic Pregnancy Statistics* http://www.en.tommys.org/
[6] *Prayer of Restitution* is available at:
http://aslansplace.com/language/en/prayer-of-restitution/

CHAPTER EIGHT
Miracles at Macy's *(Category 3)*

> *Is anyone among you sick? Let him call for the elders of the church, and let them pray over him, anointing him with oil in the name of the Lord.*[1]

It is my opinion that the least understood of the gifts of the Holy Spirit[2] is the gift of discernment. Hebrews 5:14 shines light on why this gift has not yet fully manifested in the body of Christ, explaining that discernment is for mature sons and daughters who by constant practice have trained their spiritual senses to discern what is happening in the spiritual realms through the use of the five physical senses:[3]

> *But solid food is for the mature, who because of practice have their senses trained to discern good and evil.*[4]

For example:
- King David **heard**[5] the sound of marching in the tops of balsam trees nearby, and this sound in the Spirit assured him that the Philistines would be defeated, just as God had promised.

- Joshua **saw**[6] the commander of the host as he approached the city of Jericho and asked if he were friend or foe. The commander assured him that he was of the Lord's army, giving Joshua the confidence to lead the Israelites to take Jericho by storm.
- David **smelled**[7] the fragrance of the Lord.
- Job **tasted**[8] injustice on his tongue.
- Peter **felt**[9] an angel rouse him from his sleep and help him escape from prison.

In the Old Testament, the elders were men of wisdom and insight who sat at the city gate overseeing the affairs of the people.[10] In the New Testament, the elders were, and still are today, the senior leaders of the local church who are responsible for overseeing, protecting and praying for God's people.[11]

> *Is anyone among you sick? Let him call for the elders of the church, and let them pray over him, anointing him with oil in the name of the Lord.*

The Bible also informs us that elders may also be created spiritual beings that surround the throne of God[12] and serve several specific functions:

- They worship God[13]
- They lay their crowns before God[14]
- They communicate with God's people[15]
- They collect the prayers of God's people in bowls[16]
- They sing new songs to God[17]

As stated above, one of the functions of the elders of the local church is to pray for the sick. Interestingly, one of the functions of the twenty-four elders around God's throne is to collect the prayers of the saints. Since 1996, over and over I have experienced the strategic involvement with healing of the twenty-four elders as they touch specific parts of my body, thus revealing the specific physical conditions the Father wants to heal.[18]

As Barbara and I walked through a side door into Macy's in Kaneohe, I felt a sharp pain in one of my elbows, which I've learned is the Lord letting me know that He wants to minister to someone dealing with inflammation in their body, such as arthritis, tendinitis etc. "Great!" I thought, "There are so many people here Lord. Whom do You want me to pray for?"

Meanwhile, my wife made her way toward the jewelry department where a sales clerk asked what kind of jewelry she wanted to buy. Barb replied that she was just looking, and continued to browse. At that moment, I felt the same pain in my elbow again so, encouraged, I spoke to the clerk, "I know this sounds crazy, but do you have arthritis?" Surprised, she stepped back and replied, "I just came from seeing my doctor earlier today. He shared the results of a recent MRI that indicates my spine is riddled with arthritis. How do you know?" Full of faith I asked, "Can I pray for you?" As I did, another sales clerk slowly inched her way towards us, and as she got closer I felt a flash of pain behind my right eye. Taken by surprise, I said to the Lord, "This is too much for me to figure out Lord. I'm not going to say anything."

Politely waiting until I finished praying, the second lady said, "My daughter just called and needs prayer because she was just diagnosed with cancer behind her right eye." I was dumbfounded! I prayed for her daughter's healing and told both women that my church would be praying for them as well.

A month later, I returned to the jewelry department to check up on both women. To my dismay, I was told that the sales clerk with the arthritic spine had been transferred to another store so I don't know whether she was healed or not. The other lady, however, was working that day and she reported that her daughter had been completely healed of the cancer. I asked if she knew Jesus and she said that she did and was attending a local church. I left Macy's in awe of the miracle-working power of the Lord.

One of the reasons I love to go to Macy's is that they have a great cafeteria called the Gazebo. One day, while standing in line for lunch, I felt an intense heaviness in my chest. Paying the bill, I asked the cashier if she or any of the other employees who were working that day had any health issues related to their chest. She replied, "One of our workers just found out she has breast cancer." "Can I pray for her?" I asked with great anticipation, but was told that since she'd just received the news about the cancer they'd sent her home for the day. Before leaving the cafeteria, I asked the manager to let her employee know that we would be praying for God to heal her, and not to worry. I then informed our intercessors about her condition and they began to pray for her over the next thirty days.

Months later, I received a letter from the employee asking me to thank our intercessors. The reason? You guessed it. The cancer in her breast had completely vanished. From this experience and other God-encounters at Macy's, I have learned that if you establish a place where you can consistently interact with those who have not experienced God, He will introduce Himself by performing miracles on their behalf.[19]

Macy's is obviously not the only place where God heals people, but it is the place that we regularly frequent to introduce others to Jesus. Whether it's your hair salon, tennis club or workout center; where can you go to establish new relationships and introduce others to the miracle-working power of Jesus?

After church one Sunday, six of us had gathered at the Gazebo to pray. As the assistant manager walked by I asked, "Cheryl, is there anything you need prayer for?" She replied that her entire arm, including her elbow, was throbbing with pain. Kevin, a prayer team member, queried, "On a scale of 1 to 10 how bad is your pain?" "8!" she exclaimed. He offered to pray and she gladly agreed. Now remember, sometimes God answers prayer over time and sometimes He responds quickly. This time it was only seconds before Cheryl gushed, "Oh my gosh! The pain is gone! The pain is gone!"

Every retailer knows that a happy customer will tell their friends and family about a service or product if they've had a good experience. At the outset of 2016, Cheryl had recently been promoted to manager of the Gazebo. Walking by a customer eating lunch, something told her that all was not well so she asked the woman if she was all right. The lady replied that she had been diagnosed earlier in the week with cancer of the tongue, and her husband had been diagnosed with lung cancer the previous week. Cheryl looked at her and said, "I'm not trying to force anything on you, but God healed my arm last year and the man who prayed for me is sitting at that table over there. Would you like me to ask him if he would be willing to pray for you and your husband?" "Of course!" she responded.

Kevin and Gary, another believer from our congregation, responded to Cheryl's request and walked over and introduced themselves to the husband and wife. After listening to them share the situation, they prayed for God to heal and comfort them. With tears, they expressed their gratefulness and left. Kevin and Gary haven't seen them since, so we don't know if God healed them or not, or if they have received Jesus; but sometimes our role is not to reap the harvest but to plant seeds for others to reap in the future.

> *I (Paul) planted the seed in your hearts, and Apollos watered it, but it was God who made it grow.*[20]

Although neither Kevin, Gary nor the manager of the Gazebo knows what happened, they can be congratulated for faithfully planting the seed that God wanted planted that day.

---

[1] James 5:14 ESV

[2] 1 Corinthians 12:4-11

[3] Hearing, sight, smell, taste, touch

[4] NASB

[5] 2 Samuel 5:22-25

[6] Joshua 5:13-15

[7] Psalm 45:8 (NKJV)

[8] Job 6:30

[9] Acts 12:7

[10] Ruth 4:11

[11] 1 Peter 5:1-3

[12] Revelation 4:4, 10-11; 5:8

[13] Revelation 4:10-11, 14

[14] Revelation 4:10

[15] Revelation 7:13

[16] **Revelation 5:8**

[17] Revelation 5:9

[18] I often allude to specific bodily sensations that have been felt prior to praying for the sick. Many teach that this spiritual phenomenon is spiritual word of knowledge, but I believe it is the gift of discernment.

[19] **Luke 10:8-9**

[20] 1 Corinthians 3:6

CHAPTER NINE
Test Me Again; I'm Healed! *(Category 4)*

And to the centurion Jesus said, "Go; let it be done for you as you have believed." And the servant was healed at that very moment.[1]

A young man in his mid-twenties sat across from me at a pancake house for breakfast. As we chatted, I felt a strong sensation in my groin. From previous experience, I knew that there was a strong possibility that this young man was dealing with a sexual stronghold of some kind. As we made small talk, I could tell that he wanted to tell me something but was hesitant because we were in a public place. I suggested that we could go to my nearby office for greater privacy. Once there, he confessed that prior to salvation he had slept around and had contracted a sexually transmitted disease. This was devastating because he longed to get married and go on the mission field, and felt that no woman would want to share his life because he was damaged goods. I said a quick prayer asking God to heal him. He stood up, proclaimed that God had healed him and that he was going to go back to the doctor to get retested. I must admit that my faith level wasn't very high because in my mind he had an incurable disease. Still, I encouraged him to get tested.

Several days later he explained to his physician what he believed the Lord had done and asked for a new test. Skeptical, the doctor, though a believer, tried to discourage the re-testing because he was certain the results would be unchanged. But the young man stood firm in his conviction that God had healed him and insisted. Two weeks later he called, so ecstatic that he could not contain his joy for God had completely restored his body and removed his shame. Through this young man, God taught me an invaluable lesson: God's power does not flow through parked cars. We must shift into the realm of faith and act!

In Matthew, we read of a similar man of faith:

> *When Jesus returned to Capernaum, a Roman officer came and pleaded with him, "Lord, my young servant lies in bed, paralyzed and in terrible pain." Jesus said, "I will come and heal him." But the officer said, "Lord, I am not worthy to have you come into my home. Just say the word from where you are, and my servant will be healed. I know this because I am under the authority of my superior officers, and I have authority over my soldiers. I only need to say, 'Go,' and they go, or 'Come,' and they come. And if I say to my slaves, 'Do this,' they do it." When Jesus heard this, he was amazed. Turning to those who were following him, he said, "I tell you the truth, I haven't seen faith like this in all Israel!" Then Jesus said to the Roman officer, "Go back home. Because you believed, it has happened." And the young servant was healed that same hour.[2]*

Like the centurion, the young man who had contracted a medically incurable disease acted. He put his faith into gear and experienced his Heavenly Father's healing grace. Since being healed, this young man has faithfully ministered to the homeless in Honolulu, reached out to the unsaved in the South Pacific, and has been a shining light for Christ everywhere he has gone.

---

[1] Matthew 8:13 ESV
[2] **Matthew** 8:5-10, 13 NLT

CHAPTER TEN
Set Free From the Ungodly Depth *(Category 5)*

> *Then all his sons and all his daughters arose to comfort him, but he refused to be comforted. And he said, "Surely I will go down to Sheol [the ungodly depth] in mourning for my son." So his father wept for him.[1]*

In the fall of 2015, a ministry team from our church ministered to a group of leaders at a local church. During this gathering the Lord showed me that someone attending the meeting was dealing with a painful ear condition. In response to my question about such an issue, a woman in her thirties raised her hand.

After the service, a member of our prayer team, Karen, began ministering to the lady. Closing her eyes, Karen had a startling vision of the woman in an old divers suit with a golden thread going through her head and out both ears. The suit was the old-fashioned kind with a round helmet and an attached air hose, like in the movie *20,000 Leagues Under the Sea*.

Karen shared what she had seen with me. I was puzzled and unsure of what the Lord was saying, but then had the thought to 'remove the thread from her head'. Out of obedience, I symbolically pulled the thread out of her head from the left side. Within two seconds she said, "Something crazy just happened. When you pulled the thread out of my head I actually felt it leave through my head and out my ear. I feel like I've just had surgery."

A week later our team returned to the same venue to conduct another training, and heard the woman's testimony about how she had been suffering from intense pain in both ears but was now completely pain free.

Everyone rejoiced over this amazing sign and wonder. And wonder I did, as I continued to ponder what Karen's vision of the divers suit meant. I then had an 'ah-ha' moment when I realized the suit symbolized the ungodly depth.

The ungodly depth[2] is a dimension or place within the heavenly places.[3] In Scripture, it may be referred to as:

- Sheol—Genesis 37:35, 42:38
- Hades—Matthew 16:18, Acts 2:27
- The pit—Job 33:28-30
- The lowest pit—Psalm 88:6
- The trap—Psalm 141:9, Ecclesiastes 7:26
- The net—Psalm 31:4, 35:7
- The grave—Psalm 88:5
- The snare—Psalm 124:7, 140:4
- Darkness—Psalm 88:6
- Outer darkness—Matthew 25:30
- Utter darkness—Psalm 107:10/NIV
- The land of forgetfulness—Psalm 88:12

The ungodly depth is a place within the heavenly realms where parts of a person's soul (mind, will, and emotions) are entrapped. A person can be trapped in the ungodly depth as the consequence of adultery,[4] prostitution,[5] violence, the perception that God is punishing you,[6] and a wide spectrum of traumatic life events such as a car accident, the loss of a loved one,[7] rape, divorce, a **difficult surgical procedure, and many others.**

Declarative words of a hurtful or abusive nature spoken over someone by persons in authority (i.e. husbands, parents, teachers, pastors etc.) can also place an individual in the ungodly depth.

During a visit to the church, the Lord continued to minister to the lady whose ear He had healed by healing a deep emotional wound that had been sustained during childhood. Feeling an intense pain in my chest (heart), I inquired if anyone was dealing with emotional pain. She acknowledged that it was her, and said that she was open to ministry. I asked the Lord to reveal the root of the pain and He triggered a traumatic childhood memory from a family vacation when she had fallen ill and was trying to sleep. Her father was listening to the radio, and when her mother asked him to turn down the volume so she could rest more comfortably, he adamantly objected and turned it up instead, exploding angrily at her mom. Terribly sick, she was unable to say or do anything to help her mother as her father vented his rage. Deeply traumatized by her father's mistreatment of her mother, parts of her emotions were trapped in the ungodly depth.

After her tearful recollection of the experience, one of her pastors who was sitting nearby ministered to her on the father's behalf. Speaking for the father, he asked her to forgive him for abusing her mother and not being sensitive to her need to rest. Tears poured down her face as she forgave her father during this powerful time of ministry.

I then petitioned the Lord to retrieve every part of her emotions that were trapped in the ungodly depth, and to return them to her and make her whole. Minutes later, she shared that she could actually feel parts of her emotions returning to her. She was truly overwhelmed by the Lord's goodness and mercy.

Few fathers understand the authority they carry, and the power they have to bless or curse their loved ones,[8] and have no comprehension of the lifelong effects of their unjust actions. When a person is entrapped in the ungodly depth the enemy will repeatedly bombard their emotions with fear, condemnation, guilt and shame, causing what the mental health community identifies as PTSD.[9]

So, how do you break free from the ungodly depth? There are three simple steps:

1. Forgive the person who placed you in the depth
2. Ask God to forgive you for placing others in the depth
3. Ask the Lord to retrieve all soul parts entrapped in the depth and return them to you and make you whole

Matthew 25:14-30 is an oft-misunderstood passage. In this parable Jesus tells the story of three servants who are entrusted with varying amounts of their master's money before he departed on a journey. Returning, he met with his servants to account for their stewardship. The first servant reported that he had doubled his master's money, as did the second, and he commended them both for investing wisely and invited them to share his joy. The third servant however, reported that because of fear he buried the money, earning no interest. Upset at his servant for gaining no return, the master said:

> *Throw out the worthless (unprofitable)*[10] *slave into the outer darkness; in that place there will be weeping and gnashing of teeth.*[11]

Many commentators have taught that the third servant lost his salvation because he was too afraid to invest his master's money wisely. However, the Bible teaches that the only reason anyone ends up in eternity without Christ is that they have rejected the grace of God. If salvation cannot be earned[12] why did the master send his servant into the outer darkness? Perhaps we have misinterpreted or misunderstood the term 'outer darkness' to incorrectly mean hell instead of a region or ungodly dimension within the heavenly places. David lamented:

> *For my soul has had enough troubles, and my life (soul) has drawn near to (Sheol). I am reckoned among those who go down to (the pit); I have become like a man without strength, forsaken among the dead, like the slain who lie in (the grave), whom You remember no*

more, and they are cut off from Your hand. You have put me in (the lowest pit), in (dark places), in (the depths). Will Your wonders be made known in (the darkness)? And Your righteousness in (the land of forgetfulness)? [13]

Without trying to ignite a theological debate, I am proposing that outer darkness is a spiritual dimension within the heavenly places rather than the eternal destination of those who perish without Christ. Trapped in this heavenly place, people experience torment and anguish because they have chosen not to invest the resources God has entrusted to them in the kingdom of God, or have allowed fear to keep them from pursuing God's call on their lives.

The parable of the talents is a story about releasing the kingdom of heaven on earth. If we want God to transform our nation, cities and towns we cannot bury the talents He has entrusted to us. We must get out of our seats, step into the harvest field, **and release the kingdom of God that is within us.** [14]

A man in his sixties approached me after a Sunday service, his eyes glistening with excitement as he recounted how the Lord had set him free from the ungodly depth the day before. Told by his alcoholic father multiple times that he would never amount to anything, he grew up under a dark cloud of piercing fear and self-doubt. At the age of twelve he received Jesus as his personal savior and was baptized. Six years later he experienced the person of the Holy Spirit and set his heart on becoming a pastor.

Years later, he traveled to the Philippines with his new bride, intending to launch a new ministry, but his dream to become a pastor was dashed when he was told by his leaders that he didn't have what it took to be a pastor. They said his only role would be to support leadership, but never to be a leader. Believing their words, he plunged into darkness (the depth) for thirty years; constantly questioning his identity, contemplating suicide, feeling unfulfilled and struggling to stay out of debt.

His situation turned around when one of the pastors who had dashed his hopes in the Philippines contacted him through a mutual friend. Having been previously unaware of the devastating effect that his words had had on this man, the pastor repented deeply, apologized, and spent over an hour on the phone speaking words of life over him. Today, this man has turned to a new chapter in his life. Set free from outer darkness, he has applied to a local seminary and has begun teaching a class in our church. No longer bound by hopelessness and despair, he is taking small steps into God's call on His life. Amazingly, his finances have improved too.

A former prostitute and exotic dancer sat before a small group of believers in my living room and shared that she had been a part of the sex industry in Hawaii for fifteen years. Kept from moving into her potential, and always feeling like she didn't belong in any social setting or to any church family, she was astounded by what happened after we prayed to remove her from the ungodly depth.

To her amazement, she began to receive multiple invitations to lead worship at different venues. This blessed her tremendously, as worship is her personal 12-volt battery. She has also begun to see vivid visions that have both drawn her closer to the Lord and presented her with multiple opportunities to pray for others who are struggling with various emotional and spiritual issues. At the age of sixty-two, she feels like she has been given a fresh start.

Like many Spirit-filled believers in our churches who are trapped in the ungodly depth, this woman struggled for years because parts of her mind, will and emotions were entrapped in this spiritual dimension. It's probably safe to say that many pre-believers are also trapped in this spiritual dimension, saddled with depression and their doctors prescribing medication and psychotherapy.

A ten-year-old girl came into my office with her grandmother. Removed from her parents' custody by Child Protective Services, she was placed under the care of her two grandmothers. The one on her father's side explained that the girl was having difficulty getting along with her classmates and teachers at school. She also disclosed that her granddaughter had been diagnosed with bi-polar disorder.

During our two-hour session I learned that this charming ten-year-old had not only been physically and emotionally abused by her father, but she had also been separated from her two younger sisters. Traumatized and full of hurt, she vented her anger at her father, teacher and classmates because her emotions were entrapped in the ungodly depth.

It was extremely difficult for this little girl to forgive her father but eventually, with a lot encouragement, she did and I prayed for the Lord to remove her from the ungodly depth.

A month later, the grandmother reported that her classroom behavior had dramatically improved and that her psychologist had determined that she was no longer suffering from bi-polar disorder. This was an astonishing turn-around for an angry little girl who was about to be kicked out of school.

In 2015, a woman who had visited our church confided in my wife and me that a client of her firm had viciously raped her. She now locked herself in her office and was unable to function, causing her employer to question her performance. To make matters more complicated, the rapist was the top client of her firm—someone she interacted with regularly. Afraid to tell any of her business partners what had happened for fear of losing the client's business, she tried to move forward but was unable to do so. We explained that the trauma she had experienced had placed her in the depths of Sheol,[15] and asked if she was willing to forgive the man and pray to be removed from the ungodly depth. Desperate to move on with life, she agreed. Several months later she left her company and moved to another state, and today she is a vibrant, productive woman who is living unhindered by the horror of being stuck in the ungodly heavenly realms where she had been bombarded with anxiety and hopelessness.

I listened intently to another woman share that after eighteen years of verbal, psychological and physical abuse by her husband she was about to file for divorce. Her pastor and I both counseled her to opt for a period of separation, but she was adamant that her marriage was over. With her mind made up, I sensed that the Lord wanted to set her free from the ungodly depth. Not wanting to assume this, I asked her if she ever felt fearful, hopeless, depressed or disconnected. It was no surprise that she related to all of the above. I explained that she was likely trapped in the ungodly depth and offered her the option of breaking free. She nodded yes, forgave her husband and prayed. Afterwards she shared two things: First, she felt the release of something indescribable coming off of the top of her head (her pastor felt this too). Second, she felt a spring-like sensation washing over her. Mercifully, the Lord had loosed her from eighteen years of debilitating bondage that had placed her in a dimension of hopelessness and fear.

[1] Genesis 37:35 NASB

[2] Psalm 86:13, 107:26

[3] Ephesians 6:12

[4] Proverbs 2:18

[5] Proverbs 5:3-5, 9:18

[6] Psalm 88:1-18

[7] Genesis 37:35

[8] Genesis 31:24-32, 35:39; Proverbs 18:21

[9] *Post Traumatic Stress Disorder,* http://www.nimh.nih.gov/NationalInstituteofMentalHealth/

[10] Parentheses within Scripture are the author's throughout

[11] Matthew 25:30 NASB

[12] Ephesians 2:8-9

[13] Psalm 88:3-6 NASB

[14] Luke 19:12-27

[15] Genesis 37:35

CHAPTER ELEVEN
Friendship Evangelism (Category 6)

> *Then the master told his servant, "Go out to the roads and country lanes and compel them to come in, so that my house will be full."* [1]
>
> *You are the light of the world—like a city on a hilltop that cannot be hidden. No one lights a lamp and then puts it under a basket. Instead, a lamp is placed on a stand, where it gives light to everyone in the house. In the same way, let your good deeds shine out for all to see, so that everyone will praise your heavenly Father.* [2]

As people of the light, we are supposed to let our light shine. As people of faith, we are called to go beyond the comfort and safety of the four walls of our church structures and destroy the works of the devil.[3] Faith is private, but it is also public. We are the living body of Christ and are anointed to do greater works.[4]

People had just emptied the church parking lot and gone home, when a Dominoes Pizza delivery woman stepped out of her car and approached me:

"Are you the one who ordered the pizza?"

"No I'm not," but at that moment I felt a flash of pain in my left knee. "Is there anything wrong with your left knee?"

"Yes, I have a bad knee," she answered, looking at me with curiosity.

"Can I pray for you?"

"Sure."

I said a quick prayer for the Lord to heal her knee and then encouraged her to do something she previously couldn't do. She sat down on the ground and crossed her legs. "Oh my gosh! The pain is gone!" I asked if she knew Jesus and she replied affirmatively, adding that she hadn't gone to church in a long time because of three part time jobs. I explained that the Lord had healed her because He was trying to get her attention so she would return to Him. She thanked me, told me she was going to tell her friends about what God had done for her, and left for her next delivery.

Barbara and I were taking our customary Monday-morning walk through a beautiful townhouse community near our home. As we strolled by one of the groundskeepers I felt pain in my lower back. Having said hello to her many times, I smiled as we approached her, introduced Barb, and asked if she suffered from back trouble. She said yes, and we spent the next ten minutes getting to know her and praying, and then continued on our walk.

The next time we met she reported that her back pain had disappeared. Since that time, we've had many conversations and I have had the opportunity to pray for her about other matters. During one such time she shared that she used to follow Jesus when she was a teenager, going to church regularly, but that all changed after the pastor propositioned her in an inappropriate manner. Disillusioned, she left the church and never returned. On behalf of the pastor, I asked for forgiveness. She received my gesture and allowed me to pray for her. As tears rolled down her cheeks, she remarked that she didn't know why she was crying. I told her that it was the Holy Spirit calling her home.

Before continuing my morning walk, I encouraged her to return to church. I could tell that she wasn't ready to take that step but knew that the ice around her heart had begun to melt. My point here is to emphasize that as sons and daughters of God, we are called to mingle with people outside the four walls of the church and reconcile them to God, others and themselves.

> *Blessed are the peacemakers for they shall be called the sons of God.*[5]

If my wife and I had not followed the leading of the Holy Spirit to pray for this woman's back, we would not have learned that she was a prodigal daughter and had the opportunity to lead her back to God.

The late John Wimber once said, "The meat is in the street." Toward the end of 2007, my wife and I agreed that it was time for us to purchase a new car. As I was signing the paperwork for our shiny new Toyota FJ Cruiser at a local dealership, I felt pain at the top of my neck right under my left jaw. Pointing to the spot where I was feeling the pain I asked the salesman if he was dealing with an illness that was affecting his glands. Surprised, he shared that he had Hodgkin's Lymphoma. I offered to pray for him and he said okay. Why wouldn't he? After all, I had just purchased a new car from him.

God did not heal the Toyota salesman that evening, but He did give me the opportunity to share the gospel with him after he accepted my invitation to have lunch with me at a later date. Our conversation revealed that he had been an acolyte in the Catholic Church as a boy, had been hurt by a priest, and now wanted nothing to do with God or the Church. I allowed him to vent, and then shared that it was no mistake that we had met and that the Lord was trying to get his attention by showing me that he had Hodgkin's Lymphoma. I also explained what Jesus had done for him on the cross. Sadly, even though he heard the gospel, he declined my invitation to receive Christ, and eighteen months later he died. Although God did not heal this salesman of cancer, He reached out to him before he died to give him the opportunity to enter heaven as a son, for:

> The Lord...[wishes none] to perish but all to come to repentance.[6]

We have no control over who receives Jesus or not, but we can boldly present the gospel to others as the Lord leads.

Turning into my neighborhood, I noticed a woman on the street who I hadn't seen in years. I pulled up nearby, parked my car and yelled, "Hi, Dale. How are you doing?"

We exchanged small talk, and she mentioned that she was trying to exercise but that it was difficult because she had a sprained ankle. "Let me pray for you," I insisted. That evening I received a Facebook message from her reporting that her ankle was healed.

God will give you multiple opportunities to pray for people outside the church if you ask Him to. He cares about the smallest details of people's lives because He is a loving Father.

Twenty-five people gathered at Windward Mall in Kaneohe on a mid-week evening to pray for people's felt needs. We asked the Lord for His favor, split up into groups, and went looking for people to pray for. An hour later, we reconvened to report what God had done.[7] A man named Justin shared that although he was very nervous, he had walked up to an elderly woman and asked if he could pray for her. The woman immediately received his kind offer, explaining that she had been suffering from excruciating pain in her leg for the last year (she had broken it a year earlier and that it had not healed properly). Justin said a short prayer, not expecting anything to happen, but the woman looked at him and said, "I can't believe it, the pain is gone! Thank you so much." Justin was just as surprised! This woman experienced the healing touch of Jesus because Justin got out of his comfort zone and crossed the chicken line.

Years ago, my wife and I were walking on the second floor of the Windward Mall when we stepped into a cloud of God's healing Glory.[8] We didn't see the Glory, but we were enveloped by it, feeling it as cool, tingly and electric.

As we stood in awe of God's presence, He softly whispered, "Tell My people that I am at the Mall." I knew at that moment that the Lord wanted me to encourage the Church to think outside the box; that He wanted us to go to malls, restaurants and other public places so He could encounter people through us who are unaware that He is far more than a fairy tale. If we step out into the public arena by faith to share the gospel, God's promise is:

> *[My people] will lay their hands on the sick and they will recover.*[9]

If we aren't willing to cross the chicken line, we will never experience how incredibly faithful the Lord is to fulfill His promise to heal the sick.

---

[1] Luke 14:23 NIV
[2] Matthew 5:14-16 NLT
[3] Acts 10:38
[4] John 14:12
[5] Matthew 5:9 ESV
[6] 2 Peter 3:9 NASB
[7] Luke 9:10
[8] The Glory is the manifest presence of God
[9] Mark 16:18 NASB

CHAPTER TWELVE
A Dramatic Twist (Category 7)

> *At that very time Jesus cured many who had diseases, sicknesses and evil spirits, and gave sight to many who were blind.*[1]

Fifty people had gathered at our church office on Sunday afternoon for a class I was conducting on deliverance ministry. At the beginning of the class, I felt inflammation in my elbow and asked if anyone present had arthritis. A woman in her fifties raised her hand and shared that she had it in both of her hands. "Is there anyone in your generational line, including yourself, that has not forgiven others for past offenses?" I queried. She acknowledged that was the case with her grandmother on her mother's side.

On behalf of her mother's mother, this woman asked the Lord to forgive her family for holding onto grudges and refusing to forgive those who had hurt them. She also forgave her grandmother for passing the stronghold of arthritis to her. Within seconds, she crumbled to the floor screaming in agony as her right arm and hand twisted upwards. Everyone present let out a collective gasp as we watched the Holy Spirit flush out, and eventually expel, the spirit of arthritis. The Lord did not relent until her arm and entire body went limp. Ten years later the woman visited me at my office—still completely free of arthritis.

Over the years I have watched the Lord deliver people from the debilitating effects of arthritis. In almost every instance the root cause of their affliction has been a personal unwillingness to forgive someone who had hurt or offended them, or a generational issue because someone in their family had also refused to forgive.

Our Healing Hearts class had just concluded in our home. As people trickled out the front door, a woman requested prayer for an arthritic condition in both of her feet. Suspecting unresolved hurt, I asked if she was holding onto any bitterness toward anyone in her family. She recalled that her mother, a stoic woman, had not allowed her to express her emotions as a child. "Have you forgiven your mom?" I asked. "I guess not," she mumbled. On the spot, she forgave her mother and asked God to forgive her for years of pent-up bitterness. In response, the Holy Spirit came upon her and she slumped to the floor. The following weekend she testified in church that she could do two things she had been unable to do for a long time—she was now able to sit cross-legged on the floor, and she could walk up the stairs in her townhouse pain-free.

[1] Luke 7:21 NIV

CHAPTER THIRTEEN
Handkerchiefs, Aprons and Folder Paper (Category 8)

> *And God was doing extraordinary miracles by the hands of Paul, so that even handkerchiefs or aprons that had touched his skin were carried away to the sick, and their diseases left them and the evil spirits came out of them.*[1]

In 2009 I attended a signs and wonders conference at the Hawaii Business Convention Center. On the last day Joshua Mills, the conference speaker, raised his hands so everyone could see that oil was dripping from his hands (oil is a symbol of God's healing power)[2].

I was somewhat skeptical at first, but knew that with God all things are possible. Minutes later, Mills wiped his hands on several sheets of folder paper, cut them into pieces, and distributed them to any who wanted to give them to loved ones who needed God's miraculous healing touch.

Several women from our church watched with me as Mills distributed the pieces of paper up front, but being Baptists we weren't quite sure how to respond. Among those from our church was a new mom who had an infected nipple from nursing her baby girl, and she wanted to know what I thought. I encouraged her to go for it, so that night she taped the piece of paper she had received from Joshua Mills on her breast and went to bed. The next morning she examined her nipple and it was no longer infected. All things are possible for those who believe!

Bob Koo, referred to earlier, shared with me that the Lord once led him to have a woman with a herniated disc in her neck stand in front of a projector screen while he stood in front of the projector, casting his shadow onto her. Moments later she began to scream that the Lord had healed her neck. Her reaction was so dramatic that the sick began to form a long line to get healed.

> *The apostles were performing many miraculous signs and wonders among the people. And all the believers were meeting regularly at the Temple in the area known as Solomon's Colonnade. But no one else dared to join them, even though all the people had high regard for them. Yet more and more people believed and were brought to the Lord—crowds of both men and women. As a result of the apostles' work, sick people were brought out into the streets on beds and mats (so that Peter's shadow) might fall across some of them as he went by. Crowds came from the villages around Jerusalem, bringing their sick and those possessed by evil spirits, and they were all healed.*[3]

As Bob shared this story I was challenged because it seemed so far fetched, yet I knew that Acts 5:15 clearly said that Peter's shadow healed people. Several weeks later, Bob stood in front of our congregation and asked if anyone had a bad neck. A mother of two came forward and stood in front of the church projector screen. Bob then selected a man named Sean from the front row to project his shadow on the woman. Bob then asked how her neck felt and she said that it was better. That night I called the woman to determine if she really got healed and she reported that not only was her pain gone but also her neck was no longer clicking. I have concluded that the main reason we don't see more healing miracles inside and outside the church is because of unbelief.[4]

[1] Acts 19:11-12 NIV

[2] James 5:14
[3] Acts 5:12-16 NLT
[4] Matthew 13:58

CHAPTER FOURTEEN
Cancer—Gone! *(Category 9)*

The faithful love of the Lord never ends! His mercies never cease. Great is his faithfulness; his mercies begin afresh each morning.[1]

On December 11th, 2014, Marianne Santos was diagnosed with stage-four cancer. Her physician informed her that test results revealed that it had spread to her lungs, neck, liver, breast and groin. If this wasn't bad enough, Marianne's doctor gave her only 18-24 months to live. Devastated, she fell to her knees and cried out to the Lord for mercy. On Sunday, November 29th, less than one year after Marianne had received her terminal diagnosis, she stood before our congregation with tears running down her face and a lab report in her hand, sharing that the Lord had completely healed her. Not a single trace of the cancer remained in her body!

Barbara and I first met Marianne at Macy's, and sensing she needed prayer I'd asked if she was okay physically. She looked very healthy so we were quite surprised when she told us about the cancer. When a person is facing eternity they are often open to prayer, and Marianne was no exception. I took her hand and asked the Lord to heal her. Within seconds I felt a cool, electrically charged mist flow into her and asked if she felt it too. She did.

Two months later, I revisited Marianne at work and asked for an update. She reported with excitement that the lung tumor had shrunk from 3 cm down to 1.3 cm. "Praise God! Let's ask the Lord to shrink it down to zero," I declared confidently.

Throughout her ordeal, Marianne did her part. She asked many people to pray for her healing, changed her diet, maintained a positive attitude, quoted Scripture and declared her healing everyday. She was not a passive recipient of healing, but a bold, faith-filled participant; and she is a walking miracle, a beacon of hope for people suffering from cancer. Marianne is living proof that cancer is not a death sentence but an opportunity for God to be glorified.

Cancer is a disease in which abnormal cells divide uncontrollably and destroy body tissue. There are many types of cancer, which are typically named for the organ or the cell where it begins. Some cancers can spread from the original site and move to other places in the body.[2] Cancer affects multitudes and the statistics[3] below are offered to illustrate the magnitude of the ministry opportunities all around us:

- There are more than 100 types of cancer; any part of the body can be affected
- In 2008, 7.6 million people died of cancer, constituting 13% of all deaths worldwide
- The 5 most common types of cancer that kill women are breast, lung, stomach, colorectal, and cervical.
- The 5 most common types of cancer that kill men are lung, stomach, liver, colorectal, and esophagus

Much has been written about the causes of cancer, its prevention and various types of treatment; but regardless of any of these facts, the power of prayer is astonishing. Prayer is credited by many within the faith community as the major reason for their recovery. May the following stories inspire you to seek prayer as a viable solution for this dreaded disease in addition to what medical science offers.

Those who needed prayer were invited to come forward after our Christmas Eve service. Among those who responded was a woman in her thirties who was wearing a wig, and suffering with breast cancer:

> "Do you have a sister?" I inquired.
>
> "Yes I do."
>
> "What kind of relationship do you have with her?"
>
> "I hate her!"
>
> "Why do you hate her so much?" I asked out of curiosity.
>
> "My mother has always favored her over me," she said with a disgusted look.
>
> "How do you feel about your mom?"
>
> "I hate her too!"

In the minutes following, I encouraged this woman to forgive her mother and sister, repent for her hatred toward them, and ask God to forgive her for despising them. She did this without hesitation, and then I asked the Lord to heal her of cancer. Months later, I saw her husband at the gym and learned that the cancer had completely disappeared. Sixteen years later, she is still alive and well.

A newly married woman with stage-four brain cancer stood in front of me. Her prayer request was simple, "Lord, let me live." I prayed for God to heal her and she left. Six months later, the woman in our congregation who had invited this lady to our service told me that she had received a letter from her friend informing her that the cancer had miraculously disappeared. I was blown away!

Another woman also requested prayer for stage-four brain cancer. After asking several questions about her background, I learned that her grandfather was a 32nd degree Freemason.

Freemasonry is a secret society that believes in the existence of a supreme being, including the gods of Islam, Hinduism and other world religions.[4] As Freemasons work their way toward the highest degree of their order they symbolically curse different parts of their bodies. For example, in one of these rituals they take a noose and place it over the candidate's neck. This causes not only the fear of choking but also asthma, emphysema and other related breathing difficulties. Another ritual involving the chest often results in Freemasons and their children suffering from physical issues in the lung and heart areas. When one reaches the Holy Arch Degree, a candidate makes a symbolic gesture removing their head from their body, exposing it to the hot sun.[5] Just imagine the consequences of that!

Though supposedly symbolic, the curses Freemasons decree over themselves result in a myriad of health issues. Fortunately these declarations, when renounced,[6] can be nullified under the blood of Jesus, which this lady gladly did. A year later, one of the persons who had ministered to her with me reported that he had seen her and the brain cancer had completely disappeared!

In case your wondering, not everyone we pray for gets healed, and I have always wondered why some are healed and others aren't. I have concluded that my role is not to try and figure this mystery out, but is to love people and pray for God to do the impossible. I have also concluded that if every person we prayed for was miraculously healed, our lives would come under so much pressure that we would be tempted to believe that we were doing the healing or, just as bad, succumb to the spirit of greed because requests to pray for the terminally ill would come to our doorstep from every corner of the world. Praying for the sick is simply about loving people who are caught in a whirlwind of fear and need the Father's embrace.

[1] Lamentations 3:22-23 NLT

[2] http://curesearch.org/ "What is cancer?"

³ http://who.int/en/

⁴ http://www.gotquestions.org/ "What is Freemasonry and What Do Freemasons Believe?"

⁵ http://exposemasonicblogspot.com "Exposing Freemasonry"

⁶ http://aslansplace.com/language/en/prayer-of-release-for-masons-and-their-descendants/

CHAPTER FIFTEEN
Jumping for Joy (Category 10)

"Return home and tell how much God has done for you." So the man went away and told all over town how much Jesus had done for him.[1]

A visiting pastor, Bob Brasset, had just finished praying for a man in our congregation who had been suffering from debilitating pain in his knee for many years. Within minutes the man exclaimed that the pain in both knees was gone. A week later he demonstrated in our morning service that his knees had been healed as he jumped up into the air and landed hard on the floor. He also posted a testimonial video on Facebook of himself kneeling down on one knee, while extending his other one an inch above the floor. The video went viral.

The Lord is genuinely concerned about what concerns us. He is truly a loving Father, nothing is impossible for God and:

The Lord will accomplish what concerns you.[2]

A young woman from another church requested prayer for a knee injury she had sustained while dancing. After I prayed, she stooped down on one knee to test it out. She looked up and said, "I could not do this before without experiencing pain. I am healed." Understanding that God knows everything we are going through and that He accomplishes all that concerns us is encouraging. In this instance God restored this woman's ability to worship Him by restoring her ability to dance. He is indeed a good, good Father.

[1] Luke 8:39 NIV

[2] Psalm 138:8 NASB

CHAPTER SIXTEEN
High Blood Pressure Healed *(Category 11)*

> *Wrath is cruel, anger is overwhelming, but who can stand before jealousy?* [1]

Returning to my office after a routine check up with my doctor, I was in shock! He had told me that my blood pressure was 180/100, and I could have a stroke if I didn't get immediate care. Riddled with anxiety, I called a friend for prayer and explained the situation. He said, "Let's ask the Lord what's going on."

After a minute of silence he asked if I had been jealous of anyone lately. Stunned, I replied that I had. My friend quickly led me in prayer to repent of jealousy and to ask for the Lord's forgiveness.

The words 'jealousy' and 'envy' are often confused. We envy someone when we covet his or her advantages, successes, and possessions etc., but to be jealous means we are feeling or showing suspicion of someone's unfaithfulness in a relationship. This is a helpful definition, but it fails to explain the biblical meaning of jealousy, which is 'displacement', or 'to take one's place'. [2]

When King Saul perceived that the people of Israel loved David more than him, the spirit of jealousy snared him:

> *When the victorious Israelite army was returning home after David had killed the Philistine, women from all the towns of Israel came out to meet King Saul. They sang and danced for joy with tambourines and cymbals. This was their song: "Saul has killed his thousands, and David his ten thousands!"*
>
> *Saul was very angry. "What's this?" he said. "They credit David with ten thousands and me with only thousands. Next they'll be making him their king!" So from that time on Saul kept a jealous eye on David.* [3]

When a person's identity or self-image is rooted in their position, office or relationships, they are susceptible to the spirit of jealousy. Before Jesus commissioned the apostles to impact the world the Pharisees were the religious leaders of the day. But once the apostles began to preach the kingdom of God, with signs following; they gained favor with the people, thus displacing the Pharisees from their position of prominence:

> *As a result of the apostles' work, sick people were brought out into the streets on beds and mats so that Peter's shadow might fall across some of them as he went by. Crowds came from the villages around Jerusalem, bringing their sick and those possessed by evil spirits, and they were all healed. The high priest and his officials, who were Sadducees, were filled with jealousy. They arrested the apostles and put them in the public jail.* [4]

Why was I jealous? I fell prey to this stronghold because I believed the lie that I had lost favor and position with a senior leader to another pastor. Ironically, the person I called to pray for me was the very pastor who I believed had displaced me. God is so gracious!

As for my blood pressure, I don't fully understand why the enemy had the legal right to attack my cardiovascular system, but I suspect it may have had something to do with me not feeling secure about my identity. Like King Saul and the Pharisees, I had placed my value in my position with man instead of with the Lord. Because of this idolatry in my heart I had given the enemy the legal right to attack my body.[5]

I went back to my doctor the next day and my blood pressure was 120/80. A decade later however, because of age and stress it rose to 140/95. Concerned because my father died at the age of 66 due to complications related to heart disease, I changed my diet and began to exercise. I also saw a doctor who put me on high blood pressure medication.

In February 2016, I attended a discernment summit hosted by Aslan's Place in Hesperia, California. During one of the sessions, Paul Cox shared that science had confirmed the direct connection between physical health and the elements on the periodic table.[6] [7] [8]

What is most important to understand is that all matter is made up of the elements on the periodic table.[9] Each of these elements have unique properties that, when bound together, create molecules such as our DNA, which is an encoded design.[10] When this design is corrupted because of chemical pollutants in the environment, personal sin, or generational iniquity, we are vulnerable to infirmity.

This raises an important question: Is it possible to experience physical healing when the elements in our bodies are cleansed of personal sin and generational evil, and then brought into divine alignment with our original design?

Paul prayed for cleansing of specific elements from the periodic table in our bodies, which he discerned were defiled by generational iniquity. Returning from California, I was astounded to find that my blood pressure had dropped from 125/80 to 104/74. Prior to my trip, my doctor had lowered my blood pressure medication by 50%, so I did not expect it to drop but thought it would stay in the same range. Additional readings continued to be significantly lower. I shared this new development with Paul, and he said that others who attended the conference had shared that their blood pressure readings had also dropped—amazing!

A sample prayer to cleanse the elements in your body:

Lord Jesus, please remove any (name of element from periodic table) [11] that should not be at the cellular and sub-cellular levels, including the DNA and RNA, and bring it into correct creative order in my body. Please break all ungodly ties between the elements on the periodic table and the land as well as any land areas tied to my generational lines. Please remove all elemental spirits out of ungodly time and establish them in correct Kairos time. Align every element on the periodic table in my body to the throne of God and restore them to their original design. In Jesus' name, amen.

---

[1] Proverbs 27:4 ESV

[2] http://www.Dictionary.com

[3] 1 Samuel 18:6-9 NLT

[4] Acts 5:15-18 NLT

[5] http://www.theslg.com/ "Warfare" and "spirit of jealousy"

[6] http://www.en.encyclopedia.com/ "Periodic table of the elements"

[7] http://www.en.wikipedia.com/ "What is the periodic table?" The periodic table is a tabular arrangement of chemical elements, ordered by their atomic number (number of protons), electron configurations, and recurring chemical properties.

[8] http://chem4kids.com/ "The Periodic Table"
The periodic table is organized like a big grid, with each element placed in a specific location because of its atomic structure. As with any grid, the periodic table has rows (left to right) and columns (up and down). Each row and column has specific characteristics, and all matter is made up of the elements listed on the periodic table

[9] Ibid.

[10] http://reasons.org "Scientists Write the Book On Intelligent Design"

[11] https://en.wikipedia.org/wiki/Periodic_table

CHAPTER SEVNTEEN
Ominous Spot Disappears *(Category 12)*

> *Thus says the Lord to Cyrus His anointed, whom I have taken by the right hand, to subdue nations before him and to loose the loins of kings; To open doors before him so that gates will not be shut: "I will go before you and make the rough places smooth; I will shatter the doors of bronze and cut through their iron bars."* [1]

Richard approached me at a wedding reception and said, "Pastor Rob, I recently had an MRI and my doctor says that it revealed an ominous dark spot on my left lung. He wants to see me right away for further testing." After getting his permission to check and see if there was an ungodly door over his lung, I placed my hand over the left side of his chest and discerned one.

Doors are entrances to rooms within the heavenly places, while gates are entryways into heavenly dimensions that contain the rooms. [2] [3] Throughout the Bible gates are mentioned as places where supernatural activity occurred:

- In the days of Deborah war erupted in the gates after Israel chose new gods. [4]

- When Jesus miraculously raised a widow's son from the dead He was at the city gate of Nain.[5]
- With the walls of Jericho in ruins Joshua invoked a curse that anyone who rebuilt its gates in the future would lose their youngest son.[6]

In ancient times, the gate was Command Central for the city—the hub of governmental, spiritual and economic activity.[7] The gate was also the most fortified section of a city. Every military aggressor in biblical times knew that the key to conquering a city was to take the gate.[8] I have learned from my friend and esteemed colleague, Paul Cox, that opening and closing doors and gates as led by the Holy Spirit releases the Glory of God,[9] effecting healing for those suffering from physical and spiritual conditions.

In her article, *Exploring the Gates*,[10] Barbara Parker points out that there are tiny microscopic gates in the cells of our bodies which are defined as molecules, which act in response to a stimulus to permit or block passage through our cell membranes. Although these microscopic openings can't be seen with the naked eye, every mother knows they exist because they wash and bandage their children's scrapes and bruises with the knowledge that a bacterial infection can result if they don't.

Spiritual gates and doors on a person's body can be detected via the gift of discernment. Seers have also been able to identify them. According to Isaiah 45:1-2 and Psalm 24:7-9, the King of glory will enter the gates if the doors have been opened.

So, how did Richard fare? After discerning an ungodly door over his lung, I asked the Lord to close it so the gate behind it would remain open so His healing glory could flow in through it and heal his lung. Two days later Richard went back to the doctor for further testing and, to his doctor's surprise, the spot on his lung had disappeared. Along with many others, Richard is walking proof that the King of glory heals in many ways.

[1] Isaiah 45:1-2 NASB

[2] Genesis 28:10-17; Revelation 4:1

[3] For more information, see *Exploring Heavenly Places, Volume 3: Gates, Doors, and the Grid*

[4] Judges 5:8

[5] Luke 7:11-15

[6] Joshua 6:26; 1 Kings 16:34

[7] Genesis 19:1; Deuteronomy 21:18-21; Ruth 4:1-11; Genesis 22:17; Matthew 16:18)

[8] Deuteronomy 3:5

[9] Psalm 24:6-8

[10] http://aslansplace.com/language/en/exploring-the-gates-barbara-parker-3/

CHAPTER EIGHTEEN
The Pain is Gone! (Category 13)

> *But Samuel replied, "What is more pleasing to the Lord: your burnt offerings and sacrifices or your obedience to his voice?"* [1]

Speaking to other pastors today, it is obvious that God is healing the sick in numerous ways. Many of these breakthroughs have occurred within the four walls of the church, but the Lord is healing the sick in the marketplace as well. Colin, a seafood salesman in our congregation, shared that he felt convicted by the Holy Spirit because he didn't immediately pray for his boss's back after he'd mentioned a bad injury the previous evening. Feeling this sense of conviction, he asked the Lord to give him another opportunity. When the boss clutched his back in pain later that day, without hesitation Colin placed his hand on his back and said, "Be healed!" Moments later, the boss stopped and exclaimed, "The pain is gone!" His eyes bulging with excitement, he declared more loudly, "The pain is really gone!" Immediately, he went to the plant manager and said, "Colin healed me. My pain is gone!" Colin interjected, "I didn't heal you. That was the Lord."

This marketplace miracle has opened the door for Colin to talk to his boss about Jesus. Although he has not yet received Christ, he has been receptive to prayer, godly counsel, and has allowed believers to hold regular prayer gatherings on the job site. In the larger picture, this miracle has strengthened Colin's faith tremendously because he's had the revelation that the only thing Jesus wants him to do when presented with the opportunity to pray for someone is to step out by faith in simple obedience.

Mike, a construction foreman, reported that when his boss complained of a migraine headache he offered to pray saying, "Let me pray for you something I just learned in church." His boss was surprised at Mike's offer but said okay anyway. Mike prayed and afterwards the boss said, "I still have the headache." Undeterred, Mike said, "Let me pray one more time." Again his boss said, "I still have the headache," and walked away; but minutes later he returned and said, "Hey Mike, my headache is gone!" Mike casually replied, "I told you; Jesus heals." Because of these miracles, both Mike and Colin have gained favor with their bosses and have not only continued to pray for them but have also been able to speak into their lives.

[1] 1 Samuel 15:22 NLT

VOLUME 6

CHAPTER NINETEEN
Mailbox Wonders (Category 14)

> *And God confirmed the message by giving signs and wonders and various miracles and gifts of the Holy Spirit whenever he chose.*[1]

The Bible teaches that the five ministry offices have been given to the Church to prepare God's people for works of service.[2] Sadly, the people of God have been taught that such works are to be performed primarily within the four walls of the church, but that is not the case.

Donna, a United States postal worker who is a faithful member of our church family, recounted an amazing miracle that transpired outside the church walls. Donna is an example of someone who understands that her works of service are for both inside and outside the church—inside for the believer, and outside for the pre-believer. Donna's congregants are the people on her mail route, and her ministry is praying for their felt needs.

While delivering the mail to a residence, a woman came out of her home to tell Donna that a recent medical test revealed that her arteries were 95% clogged. Donna prayed a simple prayer for the Lord to clear her arteries and drove on. Two weeks later, the woman gave Donna amazing news—much to her doctor's surprise, another test showed that her arteries had completely cleared!

During another mail delivery, Donna offered to pray for an older woman. Very grateful for Donna's offer, the lady explained that she had repeatedly asked the Lord to send someone to pray for her. Donna asked what her need was and, like the other woman, she requested prayer for blocked arteries. Donna obliged, and once again God 'delivered the mail' by completely clearing her arteries!

[1] Hebrews 2:4
[2] Ephesians 4:11-13

CHAPTER TWENTY
Massive Brain Aneurysm Healed *(Category 15)*

People of Israel, listen! God publicly endorsed Jesus the Nazarene by doing powerful miracles, wonders, and signs through him, as you well know.[1]

In 1997, Colleen suffered the rupture of a massive brain aneurysm in her home. A group of us huddled around her husband, Glenn, in the hospital's ER waiting room to offer our support.

After about an hour, Colleen's physician stopped by to inform Glenn that her condition was grave and that he should prepare for the worst.

When Glenn and I were allowed to see Colleen her face was bloated—black-and-blue, as if she had been in a brawl. Glenn stood at her side and held her hand. It was a difficult moment.

Overwhelmed by the gravity of Colleen's condition, I laid hands on her shoulders and asked the Holy Spirit to come; but to be honest, it was with very little faith. To my surprise, within seconds I felt a cool, tingly flow of air—like fog—cascade down from the top of my head, past my shoulder, and through my hand into Colleen's body.

Walking out to the hospital parking lot together I said, "Don't worry Glenn, I think God just did something. Colleen is gonna be okay."

Colleen returned home two weeks later, and is alive and well today. Nothing is impossible for God!

[1] Acts 2:22 NLT

CHAPTER TWENTY-ONE
Asthma Healed (Category 16)

> *Crowds gathered also from the towns around Jerusalem, bringing their sick and those tormented by impure spirits, and all of them were healed.*[1]

In 2004, my son, Jordan, and I went on a mission trip to Ireland. When we arrived at the church facility, a woman informed me that her adult daughter was traveling down from the Northern Ireland because she wanted to be healed of asthma.

Freemasonry and various environmental factors can cause asthma, but the most frequent cause of this debilitating disease seems to be parental arguing. When parents quarrel in front of their children they give the enemy the legal right to afflict them with a fear of being abandoned. When this occurs, a child's hypothalamus gland secretes a hormone called ACTH, which goes into their bloodstream and docks at their alveoli, producing stiffening of the cell walls.[2]

Later in the week, I met with the daughter and asked if her parents had argued in front of her as a child. "Yes, my parents argued a lot. I remember a particular instance when they were so angry at one another that my brothers and I huddled together in our bedroom shaking with fear." She then forgave her parents for quarreling and exposing her to the spirit of fear; and I rebuked the fear of abandonment that had taken up residence in her lungs, and asked the Lord to heal her. After returning home to Hawaii, I inquired about her status and learned that she was breathing much better!

A man in his thirties came late to a discernment class in the fall of 2015. He shared that he was late because he had to go home and get his inhaler because he'd experienced a severe asthma attack that morning.

Half an hour before he arrived, I had begun teaching about the root causes of asthma and other related lung conditions. As I was summarizing these points he walked into the room just in time to hear the question, "Do any of you have asthma or other related lung issues?" Along with five others, he raised his hand.

Backtracking, the previous day my wife and I had returned from a conference where we had conducted two back-to-back workshops. Exhausted, I went into our living room to soak in the presence of the Lord. Lying on the floor, I was engulfed in the burning furnace of the Lord.[3] During this divine encounter, which lasted for two hours, the Lord told me that He was going to release a greater anointing upon His people to heal the sick and deliver the demonized.

Now, with my supernatural encounter freshly in mind, I asked those in the class to stand and receive a fresh impartation to heal the sick and deliver the demonized so they could minister to the people who had breathing issues.

Within moments people began to experience the tangible presence of God. Some cried, others laughed, some groaned and others slumped to the floor. Four people who had just received the impartation surrounded the man who had come late and began to pray for his lungs to be healed. He slumped to the floor on his hands and knees and coughed for fifteen minutes as the Holy Spirit delivered him from fear and insecurity.

Afterwards, I asked him if his parents had argued when he was a child. His answer was shocking! His parents had not only argued, but they had also fought physically to the point where his mom had lunged at his father with a knife. Thankfully, because his dad knew self-defense, he was able to disarm the mother. Later, his parents got divorced. As this man shared this memory, the light bulb went on for him and he was able to trace his frequent asthma attacks to that stormy period in his parent's marriage.

To be healed of asthma that is rooted in parental arguing requires that an individual forgive them for creating an environment of anxiety, fear, and insecurity in the home while growing up, and commanding the spiritual entities that infiltrated their lungs during this time to leave in the name of Jesus. This man experienced breakthrough that afternoon because he was willing to forgive his parents for their volatile marriage and for exposing him to fear and insecurity. Today he is asthma free.

[1] Acts 5:16 NIV

[2] Henry Wright, *A More Excellent Way* (Thomaston, Georgia: Pleasant Valley Publications, 2005), 192

[3] Exodus 19:18; Proverbs 17:3; Malachi 4:1

CHAPTER TWENTY-TWO
Ears Opened (Category 17)

> *Then Jesus left the vicinity of Tyre and went through Sidon, down to the Sea of Galilee and into the region of the Decapolis. There some people brought to him a man who was deaf and could hardly talk, and they begged Jesus to place his hand on him. After he took him aside, away from the crowd, Jesus put his fingers into the man's ears. Then he spit and touched the man's tongue. He looked up to heaven and with a deep sigh said to him, "Ephphatha!" which means "Be opened!" At this, the man's ears were opened, his tongue was loosened and he began to speak plainly.*[1]

While on the same mission trip to Ireland, a woman requested prayer for deafness in her right ear. When she was a little girl she had been standing in a parking lot when a motorcycle muffler popped loudly nearby. Her right ear throbbing with pain, her parents rushed her to the nearest hospital where a doctor diagnosed a perforated eardrum. He then gave her mom and dad the bad news that their daughter would not be able to hear out of her right ear for the rest of her life. With this story fresh in mind, I placed my index finger in her ear and asked the Lord to open it. To her amazement and mine, her ear opened. It is such a thrill to watch people react when Jesus heals!

On another occasion, three women on our prayer team encircled a man who came forward to get prayer for one of his ears in which he had a 75% hearing loss. Nothing immediate happened that morning, but a few days later the man felt and heard repeated popping in his ear and realized that God had completely restored his hearing. **Jesus is the same yesterday, today, and forever!**

[1] Mark 7:31-35 NIV

CHAPTER TWENTY-THREE
God Loves Hindus *(Category 18)*

> *For this is how God loved the world: He gave his one and only Son, so that everyone who believes in him will not perish but have eternal life. God sent his Son into the world not to judge the world, but to save the world through him.*[1]

An old neighbor, a Hindu lady, arrived at my front door with her two adult sons to say hello. Vacationing on Oahu, she wanted to stop by the old neighborhood and visit friends. As we were catching up on old times, I started to feel pressure on my left eye. I asked if she had any physical issues with that part of her body and she replied that she had conjunctivitis. I asked if I could pray for her and she consented. It was just a quick, 20-second prayer and we continued our conversation. She sent a message on Facebook a week later saying that she had awakened the next day and realized the conjunctivitis was gone. I messaged her back, telling her if she ever wanted to know why God had healed her that I would be glad to tell her about it. Although my old friend has stayed in contact with me, she has not responded to my offer yet.

[1] John 3:16-17 NLT

CHAPTER TWENTY-FOUR
Migraine Miracles (Category 19)

> *It is the same with my word. I send it out, and it always produces fruit. It will accomplish all I want it to, and it will prosper everywhere I send it.*[1]

TC, a woman in our congregation, shared the following story about a nurse she had prayed for at her mother's long-term care facility:

> I had just prayed for Jackie, my mom's favorite nurse at the nursing home, after Mom told me that she had been suffering from constant migraines for the last few weeks. Although she was in severe pain, Jackie had no choice but to keep working, so I asked if I could pray for her, explaining that Jesus loves to heal people. She agreed, so I commanded the spirit of migraine to leave and for the pain to go to the feet of Jesus.
>
> "How does it feel? Is the pain any better?" I asked. "It's fine," she yelled as she began to run down the driveway. "Sorry, my ride is waiting; I need to leave; thank you."
>
> Why did I feel like she was running away from me? "Okay Papa, you just asked me to be obedient, so I'm going to

keep trying to do what I feel You are leading me to do, regardless of the outcome."

I saw Jackie three weeks later and asked how she was doing. She replied, "I wanted to tell you, but haven't had a chance to talk to you. Ever since you prayed for me, I haven't had a single migraine!"

Michelle started visiting our church on a regular basis. As I got to know her, she shared that she had been suffering from debilitating migraines [2] for over nineteen years. Chatting with Michelle, I discerned the stronghold of Molech as a painful sensation on my left knee,[3] indicating that she had ancestors in her generational line who were Ba'al worshippers. According to Jeremiah 32:35, Ba'al and Molech were intertwined, if not the same deity, and Molech was the fire god of the Canaanite people.[4] Worshippers sacrificed their children in the fires of Molech believing that, in return, Molech would bless them with a good crop, protection from their enemies etc.[5] The sacrifice of children in exchange for divine favor became common practice throughout Israel's history, plunging them into spiritual darkness. Moses warned the Israelites that if they worshipped other gods, severe consequences would affect them and future generations [6] (i.e. chronic diseases, mental illnesses, financial lack, family alienation, premature death, etc.).

Based on a previous conversation. I knew that Michelle was a Sephardic Jew—a Jew of Spanish or Portuguese ancestry.[7] Because of this, I explained to her that it was likely that Ba'al-Molech worship was a generational issue and recommended that she repent for and renounce this stronghold by praying a prayer that I helped co-author with Paul Cox entitled, the *Prayer of Restitution*.[8]

Soon after, Michelle sent me an email saying, "I have to tell you I haven't had any migraines! Even today, after going for a short but strenuous hike; which always causes a migraine for the strenuous part!!! I haven't gotten anything! Since Sunday, I've felt something that is almost like a pulling off the top of my head, and very minimal headache pain, almost like waves but never constant. I've never experienced anything like this before. Thanks again for telling me about the prayer!"

---

[1] Isaiah 55:11 NLT

[2] Migraine headaches are usually described as an intense, throbbing or pounding pain that involves one temple. Sometimes the pain is located in the forehead, around the eye, or in the back of the head. Nausea, vomiting, diarrhea, paleness, cold hands, cold feet, and sensitivity to light and sound commonly accompany this debilitating condition. http://www.WebMd.com/ "What are the symptoms of migraine headaches?"

[3] 1 Kings 19:18

[4] Leviticus 18:21; Leviticus 20:2-5; 1 Kings 11:7; 2 Kings 23:10

[5] Paul Cox and Rob Gross, *Exploring the Heavenly Realms, Volume 2* (Hesperia, California: 2014), 45.

[6] Deuteronomy 28:15-68

[7] http://en.wikipedia.com/ "Sephardic Jews"

[8] http://aslansplace.com/language/en/prayer-of-restitution/

CHAPTER TWENTY-FIVE
God Heals Through Us—In Spite of Us! *(Category 20)*

> *Each time he said, "My grace is all you need. My power works best in weakness." So now I am glad to boast about my weaknesses, so that the power of Christ can work through me."* [1]

One of the most deceptive tactics of the enemy is that he uses the first-person when he murmurs lies to God's people. Instead of saying, "You suck!" he whispers, "I suck!" The devil employs this insidious strategy not only to discourage us from crossing the chicken line, but also to drown us in a sea of lifeless religiosity. Please receive this into your spirit: God can heal and deliver people through you, even when you're not having a stellar day. If you recall, TC prayed for her mother's nurse to be healed of migraine headaches with a miraculous result. Following is another account of how God moved through TC to heal someone even though she was having a bad day:

> On Sunday, the second day of a conference, I saw Lynne walk into the room on crutches. Her knee had been injured the previous month in a freak accident, causing the joint to be separated and resulting in extreme pain. I prayed for her and immediately she was able to swing her

leg back and forth without pain, and stood up straight without her knee buckling backwards.

On Monday, Lynne showed off the sandals that she could finally wear because she no longer needed crutches—she even walked around the mall four times!

When God heals, the news of His exploits spreads quickly,[2] and the next day Lynne's co-worker, Tanya, asked me to pray for her hand because she had heard what God had done. Tanya had suffered from painful tremors since birth. I was unable to pray for her at that moment, but promised to do it the next day.

When Tuesday came, I was struggling; I was tired and didn't feel like the Proverbs 31 woman the Bible says I am, so I reminded myself that all I had to do was sow seed.

When I finally got the opportunity to pray for Tanya I was shocked to see how badly her hand was shaking. I invited God's presence, and He immediately showed up. As I prayed, Tanya felt warmth on her forearm and said that the pain in her arm was gone. With her hands in mine, the shaking started to slow dramatically. I finished praying for her, and together we thanked the Lord and praised Him for what He had begun and would soon complete.

Overwhelmed and near tears, Tanya shared that she hadn't felt such peace in a long time. Thank goodness God helped me overcome my shortcomings that day, and thank God we don't need to have it all together for Him to work through us.

When we feel unqualified:

> *Remember, dear brothers and sisters, that few of you were wise in the world's eyes or powerful or wealthy when God called you. Instead, God chose things the world considers foolish in order to shame those*

who think they are wise. And he chose things that are powerless to shame those who are powerful.[3]

TC's story is a good reminder that we don't have to have it together for God to work through us on behalf of others. Feeling good, strong or adequate are not prerequisites for us to be qualified as vessels through whom the Lord moves. The only thing required is a willing heart.

[1] 2 Corinthians 12:9 NLT
[2] Matthew 4:24
[3] 1 Corinthians 1:26-27 NLT

CHAPTER TWENTY-SIX
A Buddhist Couple Turns to Jesus (Category 21)

> *And the hand of the Lord was with them, and a great number who believed turned to the Lord.*[1]

On a midweek evening, a group of intercessors gathered at our church office to pray. They arrived with one purpose in mind—to petition God to reveal Himself to their friends and loved ones. Among those present were my son, Brandon, and his fiancé, Michelle. As the evening unfolded, the Spirit of God fell on Brandon and Michelle and they began to weep before the Lord on behalf of Michelle's parents, Mike and Susan. Several weeks later, the Lord answered their heartfelt prayers as Michelle's parents surrendered their lives to Jesus.

This may not seem out of the ordinary, but Buddhists rarely turn to Jesus in Hawaii. These are wonderful people who faithfully honor their deceased ancestors at local temples and burn incense at family altars in their homes. Typically, when presented with the Gospel they are not open because the enemy has blinded them from seeing their need for Christ. Also, they see Christianity strictly as a western religion. Whatever the reason, Buddhists do not often accept Jesus. This is why heartfelt, sustained prayer for them is vital.

Today, Mike and Susan are among the most faithful members of our church family. They serve on our prayer team and Mike oversees our Sunday set-up ministry. Prayer does not make a difference; it is the difference!

[1] Acts 11:21 ESV

CHAPTER TWENTY-SEVEN
Children Do Not Have a 'Junior' Holy Spirit
(Category 22)

> *Let the children come to me; do not hinder them, for to such belongs the kingdom of God.*[1]

It was a sunny day on the bunny slope at the Park City ski resort. It was 1978, my first experience skiing, and I was terrified of falling but was determined to go for it!

Like most newbies, I fell over and over until I slowly got the hang of traversing back and forth, employing the snowplow technique. Lumbering down the bunny slope, I was amazed and embarrassed as little children two to four years of age swept past, leaving me wondering how they caught on so fast. As I continued to watch these future Olympians easily navigate their way down the slope, it dawned on me. The reason they were able to master the basics so quickly was because they had no fear of falling.

Every third Sunday, our church invites our ten-year-olds to help us pray for the sick. Over the years the Lord has shown us that His precious little ones do not have a junior Holy Spirit. Like the little kids who went for it on skis, ten-year-olds pray for the sick with childlike confidence. One Sunday in 2015, a girl prayed for a woman in our church who was complaining of a frozen shoulder. If you have ever had a shoulder ailment of any kind you understand the challenges, including difficulty sleeping at night, limited range of motion, and feeling grumpy 24/7 because your muscles and tendons feel constantly inflamed, and you can commiserate with this lady!

The little girl prayed a short prayer and to the woman's amazement, the shoulder pain disappeared; and to this day it is still gone. A week later I interviewed the little girl during the service and asked what she prayed for. Innocently, she replied, "I don't remember."

Traversing in kingdom power requires simple childlike faith. We adults have to figure everything out before we go for it, but children just do it because they don't know they can't.

[1] Mark 10:14 ESV

CHAPTER TWENTY-EIGHT
The Fireman's Boot (Category 23)

> *When they reached the place God had told him about, Abraham built an altar there and arranged the wood on it. He bound his son Isaac and laid him on the altar, on top of the wood. Then he reached out his hand and took the knife to slay his son. But the angel of the Lord called out to him from heaven, "Abraham! Abraham!" "Here I am," he replied. "Do not lay a hand on the boy," he said. "Do not do anything to him. Now I know that you fear God, because you have not withheld from me your son, your only son." Abraham looked up and there in a thicket he saw a ram caught by its horns. He went over and took the ram and sacrificed it as a burnt offering instead of his son. So Abraham called that place The Lord Will Provide. And to this day it is said, "On the mountain of the Lord it will be provided."* [1]

It was a normal summer afternoon as I walked into our kitchen to grab an evening snack. Passing through the living room, I felt a strong sensation on the upper part of my left calf. Hungry, I ignored the sensation and headed to the fridge. After devouring my snack I walked back through the living room toward my bedroom and felt the same sensation again. Having learned through the years to pay careful attention to what the Lord is saying to me via physical discernment, I now simply asked Him, "Lord, what are You saying?" So I sat down in my living room and waited on the Lord. An odd thought then came, "It's an angel of provision." I didn't think I could be hearing correctly so I went to my wife and asked her to seek the Lord, without first sharing what I thought I'd heard. She paused and said, "I heard the word, 'finance'." At this point, the Lord had my full attention!

The next day we were scheduled to hang out with two of our associate pastors, Joel and Michelle Weaver. I explained to the Weavers that the Lord had shared something new with us the previous evening and that we were seeking confirmation. I asked Michelle, a gifted seer, if she would ask the Lord to visually confirm what He had said to us. Michelle closed her eyes and said, "This is crazy; I'm sure this is off. I see a boot coming up to the top part of a person's calf and it's stuffed with cash." Stunned, I blurted, "No way! That's what God showed us too!" and with great excitement I shared what the Lord had divulged the previous evening. We were all in awe. Interestingly, firemen actually do collect money in an empty fireman's boot for charitable causes! [2]

Over the next three months, multiple individuals blessed my wife and I with over $15,000. One individual gave us $10,000 so we could take a much-needed family vacation. Matthew 6:33 promises that if we seek God and His righteousness all things will be added to us, while Philippians 4:18 tells us that God will supply all of our needs according to the riches of His glory in Christ Jesus. Later that year, Barb and I took our three sons to Disneyland and had a wonderful time together because of the Lord's gracious provision. Now, every time a provision angel shows up I know God is about to bless us or someone else financially.

Several years later I sat across the table from two other pastors at a graduation party. They explained that their church had fallen on hard times and they had not received a paycheck in six months! As they shared their plight, I sensed the provision angel manifest. Deborah, a prophetic intercessor, was also at the party; so without explaining what I was sensing, I asked her to close her eyes to check if she could see anything. To my amazement she said, "I see two hands, both filled with cash."

Filled with anticipation, I explained to the pastors how the Lord had provided for my wife and I years earlier, and shared that the same angel that had provided for us was present. I offered to pray for them and they obliged. The following week my administrative assistant received a phone call from the pastor's wife. Excited, she gushed that she and her husband had just received a sizable check in the mail, along with two round-trip airline tickets so they could attend a pastor's conference on the mainland.

One of God's many names is Jehovah Jireh. This Hebrew name for God literally means 'God is provision' or 'the God who sees'.[3] God sees our need before we ask Him for help and provides. He IS our provision.

[1] Genesis 22:9-14 NIV

[2] http://Bakersfield.com/ "Why firefighters boot-filling isn't panhandling"

[3] http://en.Bible.org/ "The Compound Names of Jehovah: Jireh, Rapha, Nissi"

CHAPTER TWENTY-NINE
A Miracle on Maui (Category 24)

> *Those who accepted his message were baptized, and about three thousand were added to their number that day.*[1]

I served as the chaplain of the Castle High School Junior Varsity and Varsity baseball teams for six years with a twofold motivation: First, I wanted to bless my community and second, I wanted to watch my son, Brandon, who was on the team. During my tenure as the team chaplain I had multiple opportunities to forge friendships with the players and their parents, pray for their felt needs and share the Gospel. In April 2006, the Lord opened the head coach's heart and he received Christ at our church office. We had opened our facility to the team as a place for the boys to do their homework at night and get tutoring for math. All seemed to be going well that year until one of the star players got into a heated disagreement with the head coach in early May just before the divisional playoffs. Thankfully, God moved and the coach and his star player patched things up. As far as the season was going however, it didn't look like we would advance to the league playoffs because we needed to win a game against an opponent that had beaten us 22-6 in the pre-season.

The day before this crucial game, something strange occurred. Large welts broke out all over my son's body. The head trainer was very concerned and suggested that my son should not play in the game the next day, stating that in all his days as a trainer he had never seen anything like this. At that moment the Lord whispered to me, "Don't worry about Brandon, Rob. The welts on his body are a sign in the physical of what I am about to do in the spiritual—a breakthrough." But, I wondered, how would I explain that to Coach Joe and the team trainer?

Deciding to step out by faith and risk looking crazy, I went to the trainer and head coach and shared what the Lord had told me. Amazingly, this satisfied them both and they decided to let Brandon play.

The next day, before the game at our opponents' field I asked the boys how many of them wanted to go to the state tournament on Maui. Only one player, a second string outfielder named Patrick, raised his hand. "I want to go!" he said enthusiastically.

Because the boys had been so badly beaten by their opponent in the pre-season, few of them believed they could win the game let alone qualify for the state playoffs. They would not only have to win this game but an additional one against an even tougher team as well.

Facing a wall of unbelief, I took a deep breath and declared, "God has shown me that the welts that broke out all over Brandon's body yesterday were a sign that you are going to have a breakthrough game today and make it to the state tournament! How many of you believe this?" One by one the boys raised their hands. "Okay Lord," I thought, "Please come through or I'm going to look like an idiot."

The game began. Energized by faith, the boys jumped out to 2-0 lead and then took a tenuous 5-0 lead into the seventh and final inning. In the bottom half of this inning, the home team stormed back to make it a 5-4 game. At this point, I could feel the tension in the air. If we lost the game we were done for the season. The opposing team was about to come up to bat and their confidence was surging. I gathered all the boys on the bench behind the dugout to pray. Each player took off his hat and took a knee. I declared, "We're going to Maui. Just believe." We prayed, and then turned our attention back to the field. I watched nervously as the batters hit three successive long fly balls into the outfield for the final three outs. Game over! We had contended for our breakthrough and had come out victorious.

When the last fly ball was caught the players exploded onto the field with shouts of joy, pumping their fists into the air. We gathered in a circle in right field with our heads bowed before the Lord. I was holding the head coach's hand and could feel his entire body trembling. I said to the team with a sigh of relief, "I told you, God would help us break out today. We're going to the state tournament!"

The next week, as we prepared for the final game that would catapult us into the state tournament, I heard a starting pitcher—one of the toughest kids on the team—singing to himself, "Brandon Gross is a sign. We're going to the state tournament, we're going to the state tournament." I was astounded. The kids believed that God was behind them.

In the next game we faced one of the best pitchers in our league. It didn't matter. The boys' faith level was so high there was no way they were going to loose. And sure enough, they won the game; placing them as the 12th and final seed in the state tournament. A week later, as my wife and I walked through the Hawaii inter island terminal to board our plane for Maui, a KHON TV news crew approached and asked us if they could interview us about the price war going on between several local airline carriers. We obliged and were on the six o'clock news that evening.

As we walked away from the reporter and her cameraman, I asked Barb, "What was that about?" I then heard the Lord clearly say, "I'm gonna put the team on the news."

It was a beautiful morning as we were about to face Maui High School in the state tournament opener at their field. The lineups were set and the umpire was about to declare, "Play ball!" when our team's assistant coach collapsed face down on the ground. Our team mom, a registered nurse, rushed to his side, took his pulse and felt nothing. He had died instantly of a heart attack. The opposing team's trainer administered cardiopulmonary resuscitation, but the coach lay motionless. The boys sobbed in shock and disbelief because they loved Coach Brent.

All year I had encouraged these young men to pray before every game and trust God. Wanting to bring calm to the boys, I gathered them around Coach Brent to pray. To our utter shock, several minutes later he started to breathe again. God had performed a miracle! I asked the team mom later if the coach had actually died, and she responded, "He had no pulse. He was dead."

After an ambulance whisked Coach Brent off to a local hospital, the umpires asked Coach Joe if we still wanted to play—the other option being to forfeit the game—and he submitted the question to the boys. Even though they were emotionally drained, their spirits were high because Coach Brent had come back to life. They chose to play and went on to defeat Maui High 1-0 as our starting pitcher threw a no-hitter. The next day, the front page of the Maui News sports section reported the no-hit, 1-0 victory, and the boys kneeling in prayer for Coach Brent. The article stated that he had collapsed dead of a heart attack but had regained consciousness. True to His word, God had put the team on the news.

Later that afternoon I visited Coach Brent at the hospital and I asked if he knew what had happened. He did not, so I shared what had transpired and how the Lord had brought him back to life. Within minutes he received Jesus into his heart as his personal Lord and Savior.

That evening our team was scheduled to face the number one seed in the tournament. On a hunch, Coach Joe decided to start a sophomore who had just been called up from the junior varsity as his starting pitcher. As this young man took the mound that night at Maui War Memorial stadium in front of a large crowd I shouted, "Pulama, the Lord is with you!" He looked back at me, nodded, and proceeded to throw a 3-0 shutout. I couldn't believe it. We had just beaten the top seed 3-0 with a sophomore pitcher on the mound.

After the game, I sensed spiritual elders on the back of my head. Remember, the twenty-four elders around God's throne collect our prayers in large bowls in the heavenly places until they are full, at which point they are tipped over as answered prayer. [2] For months prior to the state tournament, our intercessors had prayed daily for each player on the team and the coaches to receive Jesus as their Lord and Savior. When I sensed the elders on the back of my head I heard the Lord say, "The bowls have tipped over. Lead the boys to Me."

On a large grassy area at the side of the stadium, I reminded the boys that night what the Lord had done in the previous two weeks and that there could be no doubt that He is real. I asked them if they wanted to receive Jesus into their hearts and all twenty boys raised their hands to receive Him! It was a surreal moment. I finally understood why the Lord had opened the door for me to be the chaplain of the team years before.

The following evening we lost in the semi-finals to the defending champion, 5-3—not too bad for a team that wasn't even supposed to be in the tournament. Sadly, years later both coaches died of heart attacks. At Coach Brent's funeral one of his friends shared how he loved to attend Bible study. I presided over Coach Joe's funeral and shared the story above. I know I will see both men in heaven, and I will forever be in awe of the miracles the Lord did during those two weeks in the spring of 2006.

[1] Acts 2:41 NIV

[2] Revelation 4:4,10; 5:8; 8:3-5

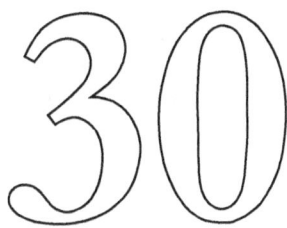

CHAPTER THIRTY
Barren No More (Category 25)

> *Therefore the Lord waits to be gracious to you, and therefore he exalts himself to show mercy to you.*[1]

Fourteen years ago I joined a group of pastors and marketplace leaders at the Blaisedell Center in Honolulu to discuss city reaching. After the meeting concluded one of the pastor's wives asked for prayer, explaining that she and her husband wanted children but were unable to conceive. Knowing that she was Chinese, I asked her if anyone in her family worshipped Kwan Yin. She acknowledged that her mother did and that a statue of the deity was still in her mother's home.

Kwan Yin is the most beloved of all Eastern goddess figures and is believed to give freely of unending sympathy, fertility, health and magical insight to all who ask. Her sacred duty is to relieve suffering and to encourage enlightenment among humans. In Eastern mythology, a rainbow bore Kwan Yin to heaven in human form. Her name, meaning 'regarder of sounds', implies that she hears the cries and prayers of the world. If you hope to have children or wish to invoke Kwan Yin's blessing and protection on the young ones in your life, you can follow Eastern custom and leave an offering for Kwan Yin of sweet cakes, lotus incense, fresh fruit and/or flowers. [2]

I explained to this pastor's wife that her mother's worship of Kwan Yin was the possible cause of her inability to conceive. She repented and renounced the worship of Kwan Yin on behalf of her mother and her mother's family line. I then prayed for her and her husband to conceive their first child. Today they have two beautiful daughters; and Jesus, not Kwan Yin, is their God of mercy!

Years later, another pastor set up an appointment for me to pray for a pastor on his staff who had nose cancer. Observing that his associate was Chinese, I inquired as in the previous story if he or anyone else in his family worshipped this idol. Like the pastor's wife, he said yes and then shared something startling. When he went to see an oncologist about his condition, the doctor told him that the majority of his male Chinese patients had nose cancer. I shared what the Lord had revealed about Kwan Yin worship and submitted that this could possibly be the root cause of the cancer. His senior pastor was skeptical, but he said that what I shared resonated with him. He gladly repented and renounced this bodhisattva[3] in his family line, and I commanded the cancer to leave. Seven years later I ran into him and he told me he was completely cancer free!

The medical community spends millions of dollars every year trying to solve the riddle of cancer. If they simply acknowledged the Great Physician and His ability to unlock the spiritual mysteries behind this terrible disease they would see far greater results.

---

[1] Isaiah 30:18 ESV

[2] http://www.journeyingtothegoddess.wordpress.com

[3] A follower of Buddha who is on the path to Awakening

CHAPTER THIRTY-ONE
Unexpected Breakthroughs *(Category 26)*

> *And David came to Baal-perazim, and David defeated them there. And he said, "The Lord has broken through my enemies before me like a breaking flood." Therefore the name of that place is called Baal-perazim.*[1]

On a Friday afternoon in March 2016, I was sitting in my living room, just hanging out with my oldest son and his wife, Jordan and Stephanie, when I felt a strong sensation on my right eye. In an adjacent room my 90-year old mother was being attended to by her home care nurse. Curious, I asked my mother's nurse, "Do you have anything affecting your right eye?" She replied with a smile on her face, "Why are you asking?" I said, "Sometimes God reveals physical conditions that people are struggling with so I can pray for them and they can be healed." She paused for a moment and replied, "My vision is blurry in my right eye and feels sore and irritated right now." I walked into the living room and sat down across from her. After spending some time getting to know her I learned that she was a Christian and received permission to pray for her.

The following Monday she informed me that her vision was no longer blurry and that the irritation in her eye had cleared. She added that she had been basking in the Lord's love all weekend and had called all of her friends to tell them what God had done for her.

Jesus prophetically declared that God's people would lay their hands on the sick and they would be healed.[2] He also stated that the family of God would not only do the same works that He was doing but also greater works.[3] The question I have is, "Do we believe Jesus at His word when He said we would do greater works than He, or do we believe the lie that God is no longer doing miracles?"

It was a Sunday afternoon in early March 2016, and I had almost finished teaching about the gift of discernment when I felt a sensation envelop the entire top left side of my head. This was a familiar sensation and I knew the Lord wanted me to introduce the revelation of a place within the heavenly realms called the library.

In the natural, a library is a collection of sources of information and similar resources that are made accessible to a defined community for reference or borrowing. It provides physical or digital access to material, and may be a physical building or room, or a virtual space, or both. A library's collection can include books, periodicals, newspapers, manuscripts, films, maps, prints, documents, microform, CDs, cassettes, videotapes, DVDs, Blu-ray Discs, e-books, audiobooks, databases, and other formats.[4]

The first libraries in human history consisted of archives of the earliest form of writing, clay tablets in cuneiform script discovered in Sumer, with some dating back to 2600 B.C. Much later, private or personal libraries composed of written books appeared in classical Greece in 5th century B.C. [5]

Although the word 'library' is not mentioned in the Bible, there is ample scriptural reference that written materials such as books, scrolls, parchments etc. could have been kept in either an actual or heavenly library.[6] Ezra mentions the book of records:

> Now because we receive support from the palace, it was not proper for us to see the king's dishonor; therefore we have sent and informed the king, that search may be made in the book of the records of your fathers. And you will find in the book of the records and know that this city is a rebellious city, harmful to kings and provinces, and that they have incited sedition within the city in former times, for which cause this city was destroyed.[7]

These verses from the book of Ezra prove that libraries did indeed exist during biblical times, but does Scripture support the possibility that a spiritual library exists in the heavenly places?

In Job 13:23-26 (NKJV) we find a thought provoking passage:

> How many are my iniquities and sins? Make me know my transgression and my sin. Why do You hide Your face, and regard me as Your enemy? Will You frighten a leaf driven to and fro? And will You pursue dry stubble? For You write bitter things against me, and make me inherit the iniquities of my youth.

These verses indicate that God recorded, and stored somewhere in heaven, Job's sin and the iniquity of his ancestors.

Another thought: Is there an ungodly library in the heavenly places where the enemy records legal rights he can use against us because of iniquity in our generational line? Yes, there is such a place:

> He (Jesus) canceled the record of the charges against us and took it away by nailing it to the cross.[8]

Back to the discernment class: After sensing the library, I threw out the question, "Has anyone here struggled with a condition or situation where they have not been able to break through for some time?" A very gifted woman who used to work for Apple shared that she had not been able to find a job though she was well qualified, and could not understand why no one wanted to hire her. I invited her to come forward and asked the Lord to go into the heavenly library and reveal the legal right of the enemy to hinder this woman from getting a job. Forty of us waited on the Lord to reply.

A few minutes later a woman shared that she'd just had a vision and wondered if it was relevant. I asked her to share it and she said that she had seen in the Spirit a group of people shackled together ankle to ankle. The thought came to me that the vision was about slavery and two questions popped into my spirit: Was the woman having difficulty finding a job because her ancestors had been enslaved? Or, was the woman struggling to find employment because her ancestors were slave owners? I asked which scenario might apply to her family. She prayed and replied, "I think my ancestors were slave owners." With nothing to lose, I suggested that she repent for and renounce the ownership of slaves in her family line. She willingly did, and immediately shared that something began to lift off the top of her head. The next day I received a Facebook message informing me that she had been offered not one, but two, jobs. Today she is employed and is basking in the grace of God. The Lord says:

I will accomplish what concerns you.[9]

What concerned this highly gifted, incredibly talented woman was that she could not, for some inexplicable reason, find a job to support herself. Aware of this, the Lord provided the necessary revelation, which was stored in the heavens, for her to experience breakthrough and to be presented with the employment options she needed. You can't make this stuff up!

Paul Cox contends that the heavenly library may function as a repository of all that is thought and said, not only by a person but also by those in their family's generational line. He also believes that the original design that is found in the DNA and RNA of each person may be contained in the library too.

What if the library in heaven is like a library in a computer operating system, in contrast to the traditional library that we think of? And, what if, generational iniquity is like a computer virus that releases the wrong instructions in a person's life? How is a computer virus dismantled? By deleting the wrong files, or changing the wrong instructions because the library in a computer system is a group of pathways containing folders, files and instructions. To rectify something that is not working correctly in a computer, computer technicians must identity the faulty folders, and delete them so the proper instructions can flow.

When we repent for and renounce our sin[10] and the sin of our ancestors[11] do we delete the files that have been giving the enemy the legal right to ravage our lives? The challenge we often face is that we don't know what legal rights or faulty folders the enemy is holding in the ungodly library. The record of debts against us has been nullified on the cross[12] but each must be taken to the cross and put to death[13] as they are revealed. Is it possible that the Lord wants to help us pinpoint or identify the faulty folders containing the wrong instructions in people's generational lines so we can bring these ungodly viruses to death on the cross and experience supernatural breakthrough?

God desires to release His manifold, multi-faceted wisdom, His solutions for people's breakthrough, through the Church;[14] and that means through us! With this truth in mind, it is not far fetched that the Lord would bring forth the revelation of the heavenly library to help us help others break through.

[1] 2 Samuel 5:20 ESV

[2] Mark 16:18

[3] John 14:12

[4] http://www.en.wikipedia.com/ "Library"

[5] Ibid.

[6] Ezra 4:14-15; Ezekiel 2:9-10, 3:1-3; Job 13:26, 31:35; Psalm 139:16; Malachi 3:16; Revelation 5:1-3,20:12

[7] Ezra 4:14-15

[8] Colossians 2:14 NLT
[9] Psalm 138:8 (NASB)
[10] 1 John 1:9
[11] Daniel 9:13-19
[12] Colossians 2:14
[13] Colossians 3:5
[14] Ephesians 3:8-10

CHAPTER THIRTY-TWO
Rescued off the Beach (Category 27)

> *After this, Jesus traveled about from one town and village to another, proclaiming the good news of the kingdom of God. The Twelve were with him, and also some women who had been cured of evil spirits and diseases: Mary called Magdalene from whom seven demons had come out; Joanna the wife of Chuza, the manager of Herod's household; Susanna; and many others.*[1]

In 1996, I received a phone call from a man notifying me that his wife had just committed suicide via a drug overdose. The news was not a surprise because she had shared with me weeks before that she intended to take her life.

Depressed for years, she felt she had no other option. I begged her not to do this but she could not be persuaded, and she asked me to look after her daughter, Maria, who was a member of our church family. I said that I would do so and reluctantly said goodbye.

I kept in touch with Maria for a few years, until she vanished off the radar screen. Jilted by her boyfriend for another woman and deeply hurt by her mom's suicide, she also plunged into depression and became an Ice[2] addict. Sadly, during this time she also lost custody of both of her children to Child Protective Services, and her job as well.

Sometime later I heard through the grapevine that Maria was living on the beach. One afternoon my wife and I were driving along Ala Moana Boulevard near Waikiki and spotted a woman we thought might be Maria at a distance. I wondered how I could get in touch with her and put the word out that I wanted to contact Maria, and we prayed. The Lord answered, and she called and agreed to meet at Windward Mall for dinner. After dinner I asked if she was willing to receive prayer at the church office from my secretary and me. She gladly agreed.

At the office we prayed that the Lord would bless Maria, help her get her children back, and get a job. To our surprise, the Lord had other plans as He began to flush out the spirit that held Maria captive to drugs, and she began to shriek very loudly. It was an experience similar to the time that Jesus confronted and cast out an evil spirit that was keeping a man in spiritual bondage. The same spiritual phenomena also occurred in Samaria when the followers of Jesus began to spread His message beyond Jerusalem:

> *The impure spirit shook the man violently and came out of him with a shriek.*[3]

> *Those who had been scattered preached the word wherever they went. Philip went down to a city in Samaria and proclaimed the Messiah (Christ) there. When the crowds heard Philip and saw the signs he performed, they all paid close attention to what he said. For with shrieks, impure spirits came out of many, and many who were paralyzed or lame were healed. So there was great joy in that city.*[4]

Drug addiction is a cruel master. Government agencies and church ministries have both tried to address this terrible plague in our society through the Ten Step Program that was pioneered by Alcoholics Anonymous. Though AA is an excellent resource that has helped millions of people enslaved by substance abuse, the Holy Spirit packs a far greater punch! Maria walked out of the church office that night free from the spirit of witchcraft—the spirit that keeps addicts hooked. Today, she is living a successful life. She loves and serves Jesus with all of her heart, has her children back, is married, has earned a college degree, and is giving back to the community as a substance abuse counselor in our city. I am proud of Maria because by the grace of God she has overcome many obstacles. She is a walking miracle.

[1] Luke 8:1-3 NIV

[2] A highly purified form of methamphetamine

[3] Mark 1:26 NIV

[4] Acts 8:1-4 NIV

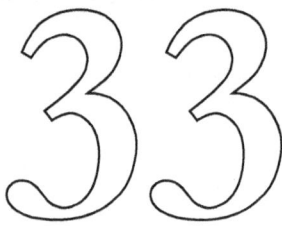

CHAPTER THIRTY-THREE
Miracle at the Farmers' Market (Category 28)

> *The earnest prayer of a righteous person has great power and produces wonderful results.*[1]

On a Wednesday afternoon, Donna, the same mail carrier who prayed for the two women with blocked arteries, went to our local mall to shop for fruits and vegetables at a Farmers' Market. While browsing, Donna noticed that one of the vendors looked discouraged. She asked why he looked so down. Looking around, he mumbled, "No customers." Boldly, Donna asked, "Can I pray that God will bring people to your stand?"

Jesus instructed His disciples to bless people and pray for their felt needs:

> *"Whenever you enter someone's home, first say, 'May God's peace be on this house.' If those who live there are peaceful, the blessing will stand; if they are not, the blessing will return to you. Don't move around from home to home. Stay in one place, eating and drinking what they provide. Don't hesitate to accept hospitality, because those who work deserve their pay. "If you enter a town and it welcomes you, eat whatever is set before you. Heal the sick, and tell them, 'The Kingdom of God is near you now.'"*[2]

Donna knew this passage, so she prayed for the Lord to send the vendor customers. As soon as she'd finished praying, she looked behind her and was surprised to see a long line of customers waiting to purchase his produce. The vendor, as you can imagine, was ecstatic. Now that's answered prayer!

As Donna shared this testimony with our congregation, she also mentioned that her heart was to lead this man to Jesus. Donna gets it. She realizes that the vendor may never set foot in our church and that she may be the only one who ever tells him what Jesus did on his behalf. The kingdom of God is not a matter of talk but of power,[3] and when His kingdom comes, the King shows up. The Lord miraculously met the need of the vendor to awaken him to the reality of who He is.

That Jesus is moving outside the four walls of the church today is not in question. The question is: Will we move with Him?

[1] James 5:16b NLT

[2] Luke 10:5-9 NLT

[3] 1 Corinthians 4:20

CHAPTER THIRTY-FOUR
Long Term Recovery Miracle (Category 29)

> *Whatever you ask in my name, this I will do, that the Father may be glorified in the Son. If you ask me anything in my name, I will do it.*[1]

A text message from Joni, a woman in our congregation, requested urgent prayer for her husband, Scott, who had suffered a massive stroke at work. Word of his plight went viral on social media, and intense intercession went up before the Lord on his behalf.

Scott's life hung in the balance as the prayers of many were faxed heavenward, and a few days later he was still alive and able to sit up in bed, albeit unable to **communicate and frustrated** by his inability to speak. According to Joni, it was a miracle that he survived. She also shared that she could feel the prayers of God's people and knew without any doubt that the reason her husband lived was because of prayer.

As we've seen, not every miracle of God is instantaneous. Sometimes He heals over time, and in such instances, Romans 8:28 is a verse that every believer needs to cling to:

And we know that for those who love God 'all things' work together for good, for those who are called according to his purpose.

In Scott's case, recovery took eight painstaking months, requiring trust in God and great patience; yet in spite of the daily challenges, Scott and Joni persevered. As Scott slowly made progress, Joni reported that he was determined to leverage his pain and learn from the experience. Romans 5:3-5 tells us that challenges and trials form the character of Jesus within us when we embrace our pain and learn from it:

> *Not only that, but we rejoice in our sufferings, knowing that suffering produces endurance, and endurance produces character, and character produces hope, and hope does not put us to shame, because God's love has been poured into our hearts through the Holy Spirit who has been given to us.*

In January 2016, eight months after his brush with death, Scott and Joni attended a church leadership gathering, where he eloquently shared that during his recovery the Lord showed him that the majority of decisions he had made during his lifetime had been based on fear instead of faith. He also shared that without the stroke he would not have had this revelation. Many in the room that night were deeply impacted by Scott's insight, and his testimony has contributed to powerful growth in the ministry of these leaders.

Unfortunately, many who seek God for instant relief from the trials they face often want a quick fix that bypasses the divine process of character formation. God loves to intervene supernaturally on our behalf, but there are also seasons when He slays the harmful demonic structures in our souls that keep us from being conformed to the image of His Son. If we are willing to die to self and allow the Father to prune us during these seasons, we will draw closer to Him and become more like Jesus in character.

---

[1] John 14:13-14

CHAPTER THIRTY-FIVE
Dimensional Breakthroughs (Category 30)

> *Then Jacob awoke from his sleep and said, "Surely the Lord is in this place, and I wasn't even aware of it!" But he was also afraid and said, "What an awesome place this is! It is none other than the house of God, the very gateway to heaven!*[1]

> *Then as I looked, I saw a door standing open in heaven, and the same voice I had heard before spoke to me like a trumpet blast. The voice said, "Come up here, and I will show you what must happen after this."* [2]

Toward the end of a Sunday worship service in November 2015, three pastors, myself included, huddled together to try and discern how the Lord wanted to minister to the congregation. Earlier that morning, Pastor Joel Weaver had delivered a powerful message about repentance. As we sought the Lord, one of the pastors saw in a vision what looked like a column of water, which became clearer and turned into a geyser. What was the Lord saying? Moments later I received a text message from an intercessor in the congregation who shared that he saw a gate in the Spirit up front. Convinced that God was inviting us to walk through the gate and into the geyser in the Spirit, we invited the congregation to come forward and do that.

As people stepped through the gate they entered a heavenly place.³ Some began to weep as they encountered God's intense love, while others experienced times of refreshing. Earlier, Pastor Joel had encouraged the congregation to repent of any issues the Lord had revealed during his message.

> *Repent therefore and be converted, that your sins may be blotted out, so that times of refreshing may come from the presence of the Lord.*⁴

Many people experienced dramatic encounters with the Lord as it became apparent that they were being shifted out of ungodly places into godly ones. An email testimony from a woman who experienced God's healing touch from childhood sexual abuse is one illustration:

> As I approached the gate, I felt heat on my feet. As I continued to walk toward the gate, I felt what seemed like fire coming up my legs. Quickly, the fire moved through every part of me, settling in my arms. When I lifted my hands up to heaven I dropped to my knees and began to scream. Instantly, I knew I had been set free from a place of entrapment as a tremendous sense of liberty flooded my entire being and the love of God filled my heart. Pastor Rob then asked me if I had been molested as a child. I said yes, and he declared, "The Lord has delivered you out of the ungodly length."

The righteous length is a place in the heavenly realms tied to sexual intimacy within the covenant of marriage. If a person has had sex outside of marriage (i.e., raped, molested, or even viewed pornography) parts of their spirit and soul will be joined to/become trapped in the ungodly length. When parts of a person's spirit and soul are held in this unrighteous dimension, they will feel lonely, isolated, or disconnected from others. The woman who shared that she had been delivered out of the ungodly length verified this when she summarized her email message:

> As I drove home that afternoon, I cried and cried. I felt so grateful for the love my Heavenly Father had just

> poured out on me. I had lost my identity and innocence at the hand of a babysitter at the age of three. I had suffered emotionally for years like a prisoner locked away in jail. Sunday, God pulled me out of that dungeon and restored what had been taken (parts of her spirit and soul) from me.

From time to time I will hear people say, "I forgave him/her for what they did to me years ago but there is still a part of me that hates them." Conversely, others may say, "I broke up with so-and-so ten years ago but there is still a part of me that loves them." I have observed over and over that the primary reason people struggle emotionally after sexual abuse, sexual activity prior to marriage, or adultery is because there are parts of their spirit and soul that are entrapped in ungodly heavenly places.

Think of the damage we could do to the kingdom of darkness if we equipped the Body of Christ to help people held in these dark places break free. We live in an immoral society where anything goes, which means by default that millions are stuck in ungodly heavenly places. We must teach our people not only to repent and to live righteously, but we must also equip them to successfully battle the unseen forces that are keeping them imprisoned.

Six months later the woman who had been healed of childhood sexual abuse sent me an exciting email:

> I received a request from a male co-worker to visit his father in the hospital. Suddenly stricken with paralysis in his arms and legs, he was unable to sit up. I visited him that evening. Standing at his bedside, along with members of his family, I introduced myself and said, "Normally, when I visit someone in the hospital I bring flowers or a gift. Tonight, I would like to give you a different kind of gift—a gift that will change your life."
>
> Having previously learned from my co-worker that his father was filled with anger and bitterness at his ex-wife, I shared how the Lord had recently delivered me from the

strongholds of anger and bitterness that I had held toward the babysitter who had molested me as a child. After sharing my testimony I asked, "If you have any anger or bitterness toward anyone today do you think you could forgive them?" His immediate reply was a definite yes! I then asked him to identity who he had not forgiven. He pointed at his ex-wife who was standing next to him, and named another family member that was not present. He forgave both of them, and I asked the Lord to restore his heart. I then asked if he wanted to receive Jesus as his personal Lord and Savior. He repented of his sins and became a member of the family of God. There wasn't a dry eye in the room. Before leaving, I asked Jesus to heal every part of his body and encouraged him to thank Jesus for complete healing. The next day he was discharged from the hospital, not only able to sit up but also to walk.

During a ministry session a woman shared, "I don't know why but I can't seem to connect to others." I inquired about her childhood and she replied that her dad had died before she was born, but her mom remarried and her stepdad began molesting her at the age of six. After hearing this horrific story I explained about the ungodly length and asked if she wanted to experience freedom. She agreed, not knowing what to expect. I had her pray the following prayer:

> Lord Jesus, I renounce and repent for my family line and myself for all ungodly sexual relationships that have placed me in the ungodly length. Please remove all soul and spirit parts that have been joined to me on the ungodly length due to being touched in ungodly ways or sexually defiled before marriage. Lord, please remove all parts of me from the ungodly length. Please gather all soul and spirit parts that were scattered throughout the ungodly grid and the ungodly length, and return them to me through Your blood according to your original design. I now declare that I will be joined only to You and to my husband. I now break all ungodly sexual ties between me and anyone else in my family line, and between myself and

any other person. Please remove all parts of me from the ungodly length. In Jesus' name, amen.

As this woman prayed, she wept as the Lord retrieved parts of her spirit and soul that had been entrapped in the ungodly length and returned them, making her whole. Several days later I learned that she was doing much better.

"How can I help you?" I asked a couple sitting across from me. "I want to be free," the wife answered. "Me too," the husband muttered. "What's the issue?" I asked, and for the next hour they angrily pointed out one another's shortcomings with stinging jabs and vicious counter punches. I repeatedly appealed to both of them to forgive one another and move forward in love, but they ignored my counsel and continued to cite past offenses. With the session nearly over, I got up and went over to them to pray a complimentary blessing so I could go home—it was that bad. I pulled the husband's chair next to his wife and began to bless their marriage. As I prayed I had the impression that I should remove some kind of spiritual device in between them that was twisting their communication. With absolutely no understanding of this instruction I declared, "Lord, please remove anything the enemy has placed in between Your son and daughter that is twisting their words." What followed was astonishing. This couple that had been at each other's throats for the last hour, tearfully fell into each other's arms and forgave one another. I walked out to my car minutes later wondering what had just happened.

A few days later, I phoned Paul Cox and shared the experience. He shared that he had experienced the same phenomena when working with married couples and explained that when a couple is unable to connect with each other it is probable that both of them are entrapped in the ungodly length.

> *For Christ himself has brought peace to us. He united Jews and Gentiles into one people when, in his own body on the cross, he broke down the wall of hostility that separated us. He did this by ending the system of law with its commandments and regulations. He made peace between Jews and Gentiles by creating in himself one new*

people from the two groups. Together as one body, Christ reconciled both groups to God by means of his death on the cross, and our hostility toward each other was put to death.[5]

When the Lord instructed me to remove the demonic device that was distorting communication between this husband and wife, the truth of Ephesians 2:14 was activated, and the wall of hostility that separated them was removed. Now able to see and hear each other's point of view, they embraced.

Recently, this couple's pastor shared that their relationship has dramatically improved and they now have hope for their future. There are still issues to work through but they are headed in the right direction. The powerful lesson I learned is that difficult marital issues cannot be dealt with by counseling alone. The invisible barriers of hostility that separate couples in the heavenly realms must be removed in Jesus' name.

[1] Genesis 28:16-17 NLT

[2] Revelation 4:1 NLT

[3] Ephesians 2:6

[4] Acts 3:19

[5] Ephesians 2:14-16 NLT

CHAPTER THIRTY-SIX
The Power of Desperate Prayer (Category 31)

> *Then another angel with a gold incense burner came and stood at the altar. And a great amount of incense was given to him to mix with the prayers of God's people as an offering on the gold altar before the throne. The smoke of the incense, mixed with the prayers of God's holy people, ascended up to God from the altar where the angel had poured them out. Then the angel filled the incense burner with fire from the altar and threw it down upon the earth; and thunder crashed, lightning flashed, and there was a terrible earthquake.*[1]

It was evening and the phone was ringing. Picking up the phone, I heard Tisha Lehfeldt, one of our associate pastors, crying frantically, "Rob, the doctor says Brad (Tisha's younger brother who was relatively young) is going to die!" I told her, "Don't worry Tisha; I'll get the word out on Facebook for people to pray. It's gonna be alright."

I hung up the phone, jumped on my iPad and posted an urgent cry for prayer on Brad's behalf, explaining that he was having life-threatening complications related to his heart and needed surgery immediately.

Within minutes, hundreds of people who knew Tisha and Brad responded, fervently asking God to intervene on Brad's behalf.

Little did any of us know as we interceded, that one of the world's top cardiologists 'just happened' to be visiting the hospital, and by God's infinite grace and mercy, he performed Brad's complicated surgery, repairing Brad's aorta from his chest all the way down into his left thigh.

Once again, when our prayers fill the bowls in the heavenly places, they are tipped over to return to earth as answered prayer:[2] [3]

> *And when he had taken the scroll, the four living creatures and the twenty-four elders fell down before the Lamb, each holding a harp, and golden bowls full of incense, which are the prayers of the saints.*[4]

Brad nearly died in his prime, but God's people altered his destiny. Did you know that your prayers can change God's mind?

> *And the Lord said to Moses, "Go down, for your people, whom you brought up out of the land of Egypt, have corrupted themselves. They have turned aside quickly out of the way that I commanded them. They have made for themselves a golden calf and have worshiped it and sacrificed to it and said, 'These are your gods, O Israel, who brought you up out of the land of Egypt!'" And the Lord said to Moses, "I have seen this people, and behold, it is a stiff-necked people. Now therefore let me alone, that my wrath may burn hot against them and I may consume them, in order that I may make a great nation of you." But Moses implored the Lord his God and said, "O Lord, why does your wrath burn hot against your people, whom you have brought out of the land of Egypt with great power and with a mighty hand? Why should the Egyptians say, 'With evil intent did he bring them out, to kill them in the mountains and to consume them from the face of the earth'? Turn from your burning anger and relent from this disaster against your people. Remember Abraham, Isaac, and Israel, your servants, to whom you swore by your own self, and said to them, 'I will multiply your offspring as the stars of heaven, and all this land that I have promised I will give to your offspring, and they shall inherit it forever.'" And the Lord*

relented from the disaster that he had spoken of bringing on his people.[5]

Brad is alive and well today because God's people fervently prayed on his behalf. What goes up must truly come down!

Prayer is more than saying grace at dinner or asking God for good weather. It is the spiritual trigger that releases God's rule, or the King's domain, into any situation.

Prayer can be likened to a thermostat. By definition, a thermometer is a device that measures the temperature of an environment, while a thermostat is a device that regulates the temperature.[6]

Because the Prince of Peace lives within us, we have the supernatural ability to alter the spiritual environment wherever we are.[7] We won't alter the spiritual climate however, if we aren't aware that the Christ who lives in us desires to interact with those around us.

Walking toward a restaurant to eat lunch with my wife, I noticed a homeless woman sitting on a bench and felt the Lord prompt me to ask if I could buy her lunch. Softly asking what she would like, her eyes pierced my heart as she responded with a soft whisper of her own, "Can you get me some orange juice and a small cup of noodles?" "Is that all you want?" I replied. "Yes," she said.

I purchased what she requested, gave it to her and walked back into the restaurant wondering how many people had walked by that day without noticing her. We will not transform our towns and cities if we do not see or care about people in need.

On a Sunday afternoon, church had just concluded and I was hungry. I drove to a nearby mall to eat at my favorite restaurant and noticed the manager seated at a table by herself. Joining her, we exchanged small talk until I asked her how she was doing. The expression on her face changed as she vented how challenging it was to find good personnel, meet company goals and live a balanced life. She was tired, frustrated and ready to quit. After offering to pray, I blessed her, asked the Holy Spirit to come and said, "Amen." She looked up with a big smile on her face and said, "I needed that! I just felt electricity go through my entire body. I feel so much better."

Remember, thermometers gauge the temperature while thermostats set the temperature. Those living the 'selfie lifestyle' will react to their environment while those living the 'Jesus Lifestyle' will change their environment!

---

[1] Revelation 8:3-5 NLT

[2] Revelation 8:3-5

[3] Jim Goll, *The Lost Art of Intercession* (Destiny Image Publishers, 2001), 39

[4] Revelation 5:8 ESV

[5] Exodus 32:7-14

[6] http://www.leadingwithtrust.com/ "Are You a Thermometer or Thermostat Leader?"

[7] Jeremiah 29:5-7

CHAPTER THIRTY-SEVEN
Until...

> And He gave some as apostles, and some as prophets, and some as evangelists, and some as pastors and teachers, for the equipping of the saints for the work of service, to the building up of the body of Christ; until we all attain to the unity of the faith, and of the knowledge of the Son of God, to a mature man, to the measure of the stature which belongs to the fullness of Christ.[1]

Some say that the offices of apostle and prophet are no longer in operation today, contending that after God jump-started the first century Church the ministries of apostle and prophet were no longer needed.[2] Sadly, this theological position has kept large parts of the New Testament Church in spiritual infancy. The apostolic-prophetic ministry is necessary for the Church to establish a healthy foundation:

> Together, we the church are his house, built on the foundation of the apostles and the prophets. And the cornerstone is Christ Jesus himself.[3]

Many understand the office of prophet, but few understand the role or function of an apostle. To clear up any confusion, let's define the term: J.D. King, the International Director of Revival

Network, provides a clear and understandable definition of the meaning of this term in an article, *Are You An Apostle?* [4]

> To understand the meaning of this word, one must also understand the growing problems in this ancient period. Rome, in particular, was dealing with a crisis of overpopulation and dwindling resources. Without additional territories for supplies and population redistribution, the social fabric could unravel.
>
> In response to this mounting crisis, the emperor sent out fleets of ships to conquer neighboring territories. These were his 'apostles'.
>
> While this entire naval armada was called 'apostolos' or the 'sent out ones', the term was particularly associated with the lead ship and its admiral.
>
> In this perilous mission the admiral had an essential duty to accomplish. While each man in the company was commissioned to fight, he was there to ensure something else. You see, this apostle was commissioned to bring the civilization of Rome into this new territory. Transforming the legal, financial and educational systems, he made sure the new land was just like home.
>
> We tend to make it a lot of other things, but at its core the apostle was simply a culture maker. He was there to make things look and feel like Rome. Through his labors, the new territory became a desirable outpost of the empire; a place even the emperor was comfortable visiting.
>
> If the apostle successfully accomplished his mission by establishing Roman culture in a new region the emperor himself would be open to visit that territory.

According to King, apostles are establishers who bring the culture of heaven to earth, thus creating a place for the King of kings to dwell. What specifically, is this culture? It is the culture of family.

The King is drawn to Church families that are raising mature sons and daughters in an unconditionally loving environment that provides prophetic encouragement, healing from orphan structures of the heart, character development and training for supernatural works of ministry in the marketplace and the world. In summary, the heart of an apostle is to raise mature, trained and equipped sons and daughters whose joy is to fulfill the Great Commission.[5]

Re-read Ephesians 4:13 ESV, and underline the word 'until', paying close attention to three specific phrases, 'unity of the faith', 'the knowledge of the Son of God', and 'to mature manhood'.

> ...*until* we all attain to the *unity of the faith* and of *the knowledge of the Son of God*, *to mature manhood*, to the measure of the stature of the fullness of Christ.

The five offices of Jesus will continue to function until the Church is united in purpose, intimate with Jesus and mature in Christ.

The worldwide family of God has come into unity over the last two decades in spite of theological differences and church practices. On April 9th, 2016, multiple streams of the Body of Christ gathered at the Los Angeles Coliseum to celebrate the 110th anniversary of the Azusa Street Revival. During this amazing event, people repented for past offenses, washed one another's feet and spoke blessings. Apostolic and prophetic leaders who understood the importance of bringing the Body of Christ into one accord spearheaded this 15-hour event. The phrase, 'with one accord', is mentioned twelve times[6] in the New Testament,[7] and is key to releasing God's government throughout the earth, for only in unity will the kingdom of God manifest in our midst.[8] The Greek word for one accord is 'homothumudon', meaning 'to lock arms with the same purpose'.[9] When we do this, we literally create a landing strip for the Holy Spirit. As we come into increasing unity with other believers, the larger the landing strip becomes, inviting the Holy Spirit to show up in even more power.

A military landing strip or landing area is known as a LZ, or landing zone. Larger vehicles require larger landing zones than smaller ones. For example, the Boeing V-22 Osprey helicopter requires a significantly larger landing zone because it generates hurricane-force winds when it lands. If we want the hurricane-force winds of the Holy Spirit to land in our midst and transform our families, towns and cities, we must expand the Holy Spirit's LZ by locking our arms together with the same purpose. Being unified doesn't mean that we have to hold the same theological beliefs or practice our faith the same way as others. Unity does require however, that we share and practice core kingdom values such as loving God, loving one another, prayer and reaching out to the Lost.

Unity also requires that we don't criticize or judge one another, but recognize, accept and support the unique gifts and callings that God has distributed throughout His Body. The Apostle Paul urged the Ephesians to:

...be diligent to preserve the unity of faith in the bond of peace.[10]

When we are diligent to love and support one another in spite of our differences, the hurricane-force winds of the Lord will land in our midst to heal the sick, deliver the demonized, and add to our numbers daily.[11] We cannot afford to condemn or criticize one another because a house divided cannot stand,[12] and a house divided will not attract the Lord's presence. This is why Jesus commanded us to love one another.[13]

In addition to birthing a unity of the faith, the Lord has also been releasing the revelation of the knowledge of the Son of God, or sonship. Jesus was not only 'the' Son but also 'a' Son. He walked so closely with His Father that He knew what the Father was doing at all times. The Holy Spirit has been diligently transitioning the Church from an orphanage into a family of sons and daughters. The purpose behind this move of the Spirit is to bring us to a place of intimacy with the Father so we, like the Son, can know what the Father is doing. Just as apostles and prophets have been working with the Lord to bring the Church into greater unity, apostles and prophets have also been busy bringing forth the revelation of sonship to the family of God. This has been necessary in order for us to function supernaturally.

The word 'knowledge' or 'epignosis' requires a quick Greek lesson. 'Epi' means 'on', and 'gnosis' means 'knowledge gained through first hand relationship or experiential knowing'.[14] Today much of the Church is driven by purpose, a move of God that has proven to be incredibly fruitful, but I believe the Lord's greater desire is for us to be led by His presence.[15]

David spoke of eternal pleasures at God's right hand,[16] referring to the Lord's intoxicating presence. Fearful of offending non-believers, we have worked overtime to make our churches attractive to the world. By contrast, King David was drawn by the eternal pleasure he experienced when he stood in the presence of God.[17] This is not to suggest that we become insensitive to the felt needs of those earnestly seeking the Lord, but that we need to make room for the Lord to move in our services as He desires. This will challenge many, but for those who are seeking the knowledge of the Son it will be life changing. Jesus taught:

> *The seeds that fell among the thorns represent those who hear the message, but all too quickly the message is crowded out by the cares and riches and pleasures of this life. And so they never grow into maturity.*[18]

What is maturity? *Webster's Dictionary* defines it as, 'the condition of being fully developed'. Jesus made an interesting statement about maturity:

> *You therefore must be perfect, as your heavenly Father is perfect.*[19]

The Greek word for perfect is the adjective, 'téleios', derived from the word 'télos', meaning 'consummated goal'; mature from going through the necessary stages to reach the end-goal or fulfilling the necessary process of one's spiritual journey. The root 'tel' means 'reaching the end'. It is like a pirate's telescope, extending out one stage at a time to achieve full-strength capacity and effectiveness.[20]

To recap, the function of five-fold ministry is threefold—to bring the Church into unity, intimacy and maturity with the Son of God.

Why does the Lord want us to become mature? It's simple—so we will know, like the Son, what the Father is doing.

John provides a perfect example of such maturity, or knowing what the Father is doing:

> *"Teacher," they said to Jesus, "This woman was caught in the act of adultery. The law of Moses says to stone her. What do you say?" They were trying to trap him into saying something they could use against him, but Jesus stooped down and wrote in the dust with his finger. They kept demanding an answer, so he stood up again and said, "All right, but let the one who has never sinned throw the first stone!" Then he stooped down again and wrote in the dust. When the accusers heard this, they slipped away one by one, beginning with the oldest, until only Jesus was left in the middle of the crowd with the woman.*[21]

What was Jesus doing when He bent down and wrote with His finger in the ground? I believe He was having an internal discussion with the Father. I imagine their conversation went something like this, "Father, this woman has broken the law. She deserves to be stoned to death. What do You want Me to do?" "Son, I am releasing the revelation of grace in the earth. Under the law all have sinned and deserve to die, but through Your example I am revealing that mercy triumphs over judgment. Tell those who want to kill her, 'He who has no sin cast the first stone', and tell My precious daughter to go and sin no more."

As we become increasingly mature we will be able to see what the Father is doing and bless those whom the Father is blessing. Transitioning into this glorious season, we will be revealed to all of creation [22] as His sons and daughters, and will accomplish the greater works of Jesus.[23]

---

[1] Ephesians 4:11-13 NASB

[2] 1 Corinthians 13:8-10

[3] Ephesians 2:20

[4] http://www.worldrevivalnetwork.blogspot.com/ "Are You an Apostle?"

[5] Matthew 28:18-20

[6] Twelve is the number of divine government

[7] Acts 1:14, 2:1, 2:46, 4:24, 5:12, 7:57, 8:6, 12:20, 15:25, 18:12, Acts 19:29 and Romans 15:6

[8] Acts 2:42-47, 4:23-41 NKJV

[9] http://www.preceptaustin.org/GreekWord Studies/ "Homothumudon"

[10] Ephesians 4:3 NASB

[11] Acts 5:12-16, NKJV

[12] Mark 3:23-25

[13] John 13:34-35

[14] http://www.biblehub.com/ "Epignosis"

[15] Exodus 13:21

[16] Psalm 16:11

[17] Psalm 63:1-8

[18] Luke 8:14 NLT

[19] Matthew 5:48 ESV

[20] http://www.biblehub.com/ "Teleios"

[21] John 8:4-9 NLT

[22] Romans 8:19

[23] John 14:12

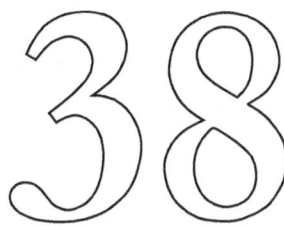

CHAPTER THIRTY-EIGHT
Closing Thoughts

Jesus encouraged His followers when He said:

> *"Do you not say, 'There are yet four months, then comes the harvest'? Look, I tell you, lift up your eyes, and see that the fields are white for harvest."* [1]

On March 23rd, 2016, three men launched a deadly terror attack upon the nation of Belgium and the international community, killing thirty-one people and injuring **hundreds more**. As news of this tragedy rippled across the Internet, the obvious message was sobering—there is no place that is immune from the premeditated attacks of the lone wolf, foot soldier, or terrorist cell group as they are able to penetrate every facet of society and inflict great damage when they are willing to die for their cause.[2]

The military tactics of our enemies have transitioned in the last two decades from conventional tactics (employing large ground forces) to small cell group tactics (foot soldiers). Like our military, the American Church is still primarily using conventional evangelistic methods to reach people (i.e. inviting people to church). Although hundreds of thousands of non-believers have received Jesus as their personal Lord and Savior in the last 25-50 years, multitudes of non-believers still remain unreached. If we sincerely desire to reach those who have not heard or experienced the Gospel, we must shift our thinking away from using conventional methods back to the way the Lord and His earliest followers evangelized their communities in the first century.

Jesus was a foot soldier. For three years He walked back and forth across the Israeli countryside healing the sick and delivering the demonized:

> *As for the word that he sent to Israel, preaching good news of peace through Jesus Christ (he is Lord of all), you yourselves know what happened throughout all Judea, beginning from Galilee after the baptism that John proclaimed: how God anointed Jesus of Nazareth with the Holy Spirit and with power. He went about doing good and healing all who were oppressed by the devil, for God was with him.*[3]

Jesus was an evangelistic strategist. He modeled a supernaturally natural lifestyle for His followers to emulate. He penetrated small towns and villages by sending the apostles out two by two.[4] In January 2016, Lance Wallnau posted a thought-provoking video on his Facebook page, *Micro Church*. Wallnau prophesied that the Lord was activating small groups of believers across our nation to penetrate society to reach the unreached. The micro church, Wallnau assured, would not replace present-day churches but would release God's power to transform lives in places the mega churches could not.

The non-Jewish world would not have heard the gospel if Peter had not visited the household of the Roman centurion, Cornelius, to tell them about Jesus.[5] Neither would the Philippian jailer nor his family have ever heard the Gospel had not Paul and Silas told them about Jesus.[6]

Just as governments across the globe have not been able to stop the advance of terrorism, Satan and his hordes will not be able to stop the advance of the kingdom of God if we, the Church, catch and embrace the vision to become equipped for supernatural works of service outside the walls of the traditional church.

As persecution mounted against the first century Church in Jerusalem, the Lord deliberately scattered thousands of believers across the surrounding countryside. The fruit of His strategy was astounding:

> And there arose on that day a great persecution against the church in Jerusalem, and they were all scattered throughout the regions of Judea and Samaria, except the apostles. Now those who were scattered went about preaching the word. Philip went down to the city of Samaria and proclaimed to them the Christ. And the crowds with one accord paid attention to what was being said by Philip when they heard him and saw the signs that he did. For unclean spirits, crying out with a loud voice, came out of many who had them, and many who were paralyzed or lame were healed. So there was much joy in that city.[7]

The early Church was not a large mega church that gathered multitudes of believers to one location, but a micro church full of individual believers like Philip, who released God's power wherever he went.

The challenge we face today is one of revelation. Will we recognize that God wants to train and equip us for supernatural works of ministry beyond our weekend services?

There are multitudes of non-believers waiting for the sons and daughters of God to arise and minister God's love to them where they live and work. The bottom line question is, "Are we willing to cross the chicken line that exists between the safety of our church traditions, practices and buildings into the world of the non-believer?"

I have highlighted some of my experiences along with those of others, who have seen the Lord move supernaturally outside of our Sunday venue to effect tangible change in people's lives. My heart has not been to criticize the Church but to encourage it to allow the Holy Spirit to set the agenda. Reading the New Testament, I see a Church that was both dedicated to discipleship[8] and supernaturally equipped to minister in power.[9] The early Church did not have an either-or mindset, but rather a both-and outlook. Today, the Church seems to be either Word oriented, without the supernatural; or supernaturally wired, without the Word. When Paul visited a Jewish synagogue in Thessalonica he cited from the Scriptures to reason with the people, some of whom were Jews; but there were also many God-fearing Greek men and prominent women who were persuaded to give their lives to Jesus.[10]

At first glance the church at Thessalonica seems to have been a Word-only church, but Paul and Silas brought the Good News to the Thessalonians not only with words but also with power.[11] Those who received Jesus as Lord and Savior during this church-planting, evangelistic outreach, were so transformed by the Spirit and the Word that they became an example to all the believers in Macedonia and Achaia. The Word was first presented to them, and then authenticated by power.

Since the time of the apostles, God has sent successive waves of revival to the Church. In every case, established churches have eventually resisted each revival as a threat to the existing structures or ways of doing things. It is time for the Church to abandon 'doing church' our way, and give ourselves completely to truly staying in step with what the Father is doing, just as Jesus did. Our willingness to radically pursue God's heart for the lost will take us outside the four walls into the streets with the most powerful revival the world has ever seen. Come Holy Spirit!

[1] John 4:35 ESV

[2] For example, the Boston marathon bombing; the slaughter of innocent people at the concert venue Bataclan in Paris; the mass shooting of people attending a holiday party at the Inland Regional Center in San Bernardino and the killing of forty-nine people in a Gay nightclub in Orlando, Florida.

[3] Acts 10:36-38 ESV

[4] Luke 9:1-6, 10; Luke 10:1-12, 17-20

[5] Acts 10:17-48

[6] Acts 16:25-34

[7] Acts 8:1b, 4-8 ESV

[8] Acts 2:42, 17:11; 1 Timothy 3:16-17

[9] Acts 2:43, 5:12-16, 19:11

[10] Acts 17:1-3

[11] 1 Thessalonians 1:5

APPENDIX

Have You Received Jesus?

You can receive Jesus right now by faith. God knows your heart and is not concerned with your words as much as He is with the attitude of your heart. With sincerity, pray:

> Lord Jesus, I need You. Thank You for dying for me on the cross to pay the penalty for my sins. I open the door of my heart and receive You as my personal Lord and Savior. Thank You for forgiving me of my sins and granting me eternal life. Take control of my life and mold me into the kind of person You want me to be. Amen.

GLOSSARY OF TERMS

Anointing: A divine grace or empowerment placed on an individual to minister supernaturally to others (Luke 4:18-19).

Asherah pole: A sacred tree or pole that stood near Canaanite religious locations to honor the mother-goddess, Asherah, the consort of Ba'al (2 Chronicles 33:1-3).

Ba'al: Semitic noun meaning lord, owner, or master; the supreme god worshipped in Canaan and Phonecia; a fertility god; involved in ritualistic prostitution in the temples and human sacrifice, usually the firstborn of the one making the sacrifice; believed to be the prince of the underworld (Numbers 25:1-3).

Bi-Polar Disorder: A disease that causes dramatic mood swings—from feeling overly high and/or irritable to sad and hopeless, and then back again, often with periods of normal mood in between. Severe changes in energy and behavior go along with these episodes. The periods of highs and lows are called episodes of mania and depression. It is often not recognized as an illness, and people may suffer for years before it is properly diagnosed and treated.

Bodhisattva: A follower of Buddha who is on the path to Awakening.

Brain Aneurysm: An aneurysm is an abnormal, weak spot on a blood vessel that causes an outward bulging or ballooning of the arterial wall. These weak spots can involve all walls of the blood vessel (fusiform aneurysm), form a sac from one wall (saccular) or separate the vessel walls (dissecting). An aneurysm can affect any vessel in the body but only those in the head can cause a serious medical condition, a hemorrhagic stroke when they rupture, which can lead to brain damage and death.

Breakthrough Gate: A heavenly opening through which captives are able to exit or walk freely out of spiritual captivity (Micah 2:13).

Buddhism: A religion to about 300 million people around the world. The word comes from 'budhi', 'to awaken'. It has its origins about 2,500 years ago when Siddhartha Gotama, known as the Buddha, was himself awakened (enlightened) at the age of 35.

Burning Furnace of the Lord: The fiery presence of the Lord (Exodus 19:18; Malachi 4:1).

Deliverance: When the Spirit of God expels a demonic influence from a person's body or soul (Mark 1:32-34).

Discernment: A spiritual gift or grace that supernaturally enables a believer to distinguish between good and evil (Hebrews 5:14).

Entrapment: Occurs when a part of a person's soul (mind, will and emotions) is imprisoned in an ungodly heavenly place such as the ungodly depths, length, height, and width (Psalm 86:13; 88:3-6).

Elders: The New and Old Testaments say that there are three categories of elders—the elderly (Genesis 50:7), appointed leaders who oversee and protect the family of God (1 Timothy 5:17), and created spiritual beings that surround the throne of God (Revelation 4:4, 10).

Elemental spirits: The Greek word for 'elemental spirits' is 'stochiea'. The stochiea are living beings on the periodic table and are essentially the basic building blocks of life (Colossians 2:8, 20) and are connected to physical healing.

Fault-finding: A demonic assignment that seduces God's people to take their eyes off of the perfection of Jesus in one another, and to look at each other's imperfections, resulting in a critical spirit (Matthew 7:1-5).

Freemasonry: A secret society that originated in the British Isles. A 33-degree Freemason is the highest level of esoteric knowledge that a Freemason can attain. Freemasons curse their bodies when they participate in their secret rituals.

Gates and Doors: Gates are entryways or openings into heavenly dimensions, while doors are entryways or openings into rooms within the dimensional heavenly places (Genesis 28:10-16; Isaiah 45:1-3; Revelation 4:1).

Generational Deliverance: Prayer ministry under the direction of the Holy Spirit that deals with iniquity in the family line for the specific purpose of alleviating spiritual and physical strongholds (2 Kings 5:27).

Gifts of Healing: Supernatural virtue of the Holy Spirit dispensed to members of the Body of Christ for the purpose of healing the sick and setting captives free (1 Corinthians 12:10).

Gold dust: A manifestation of God's glorious presence. In Exodus 12:35-36, the Israelites plundered the Egyptians of their gold. Later the gold was used to decorate the inner court and the Holy of Holies in the Tabernacle of Moses and its furniture (Exodus 25:10-18, 23-40; 26:6). Gold was presented to Jesus as a sign of His divinity (Matthew 2:11).

Hindu: A follower of Hinduism (the dominant religion of India and Nepal).

Impartation: Bestowing a spiritual gift through the laying on of hands and prayer (Romans 1:11).

Inner Healing: Prayer ministry that deals with the emotional hurts from a person's past.

Jealousy: A demonic stronghold that affects a person's cardiovascular system. It attacks those who have been displaced by someone else, such as a spouse rejected in favor of a lover. (Genesis 4:1-8; 1 Samuel 18:6; Proverbs 27:4; Acts 13:45).

Jehovah Rapha: One of the names of God meaning, 'God is healing' (Exodus 15:26; Jeremiah 30:17).

Kwan Yin: The goddess of mercy in the pantheon of Chinese gods.

Migraine: A headache of varying intensity, often accompanied by nausea and sensitivity to light and sound.

Miracle: An instantaneous healing (John 5:1-17).

Molech: Chief deity over the Canaanites, the fire god to whom child sacrifices were made (Leviticus 18:21, 20:2-5; 1 Kings 11:7).

Orphan Stronghold: A stronghold is a deeply rooted spiritual-emotional issue that has a strong hold on an individual's outlook on life. The orphan stronghold is a mindset that convinces an individual that they don't belong, must earn people's love or can't trust anyone. The Greek word for orphan is 'orphanos', meaning 'comfort less'. In John 14:18, Jesus said that He would not leave His followers comfortless but would send the Comforter to them.

Periodic Table: A tabular arrangement of the chemical elements, ordered by their atomic number (number of protons), electron configurations, and recurring chemical properties.

Seer: A believer who has been given the divine ability to see spiritual activity (angels, demons, doors, gates etc.) in the spiritual realm (1 Samuel 9:9-19; 2 Kings 6:17).

Soaking: Spending time in the presence of God accompanied by anointed music.

Sons and Daughters: Those who know the unconditional love of the Father. They know they belong in God's family (Romans 8:14,19).

STD: An infection or disease transmitted through sexual contact, caused by bacteria, viruses, or parasites.

The Depth: A place within the heavenly realms—a dimension of God's love (Ephesians 3:18). The depth is the spiritual place where our soul (mind, will and emotions) abides. The ungodly depth is an unrighteous place within the heavenly realms where condemnation, grief, guilt, and shame are empowered by criticism, sexual abuse and trauma (Genesis 37:35, Psalm 86:13, 88:3-6).

The Height: A place within the heavenly realms—a dimension of God's love. The place where we rule and reign as sons and daughters (Genesis 1:26-28; Romans 8:19; Ephesians 3:18). When a person is in entrapped in the ungodly height they will experience difficulty reaching their God given potential.

The Length: A place within the heavenly realms—a dimension of God's love. Sexual intimacy is in the godly length, whereas ungodly sexuality is in the ungodly length (Ephesians 3:18).

The Width: A place within the heavenly realms—a dimension of God's love where we relate to one another (Ephesians 3:18). The width is the spiritual dimension where love, hope, faith and trust abide. To experience the righteous width is to experience the joy of the Father and one another. When parts of a person are trapped in the ungodly width they will have difficulty trusting others.

Treasure Hunting: Going to public places in search of individuals that the Lord wants to heal and encourage.

Ungodly Trading: An unrighteous exchange that an individual makes for favor from the gods. The Canaanite people sacrificed their children in the fires of Molech for protection, good crops etc. (Leviticus 18:21).

Witchcraft: A demonic spirit that infiltrates a person's soul leading them to control, and manipulate others. It is also manifests when an individual rebels against godly authority (1 Samuel 15:23; Galatians 3:1).

ABOUT THE AUTHOR

In 1992, Pastor Rob Gross planted Mountain View Community Church in Kaneohe, Hawaii, where he continues to serve as senior pastor along with his wife, Barbara. He trains and equips pastors in other churches and spends time training God's people for kingdom service. He is recognized as a pastor to pastors, and has a prayer-counseling ministry known for releasing breakthrough and healing in peoples' lives. He has taught workshops and seminars including "Gifts of the Spirit", "Prophetic Evangelism", "The One New Man", "The Orphan Stronghold" and "The Father's Blessing".

Rob grew up in Kaneohe Hawaii, and is of Jewish and Japanese ancestry. He graduated from Iolani High School and earned his bachelor's degree and Phi Beta Kappa honors from the University of Hawaii. After working five years in the marketplace, he earned his Master of Divinity degree from Golden Gate Baptist Theological Seminary. He has ministered both in United States and abroad in such countries as Hong Kong, Ireland, Japan, Guam and Thailand. From 1997-2002, Rob led the Watch of the Lord®; a multi-denominational, monthly intercessory gathering that petitioned the Lord for revival in the Hawaiian Islands.

In 2001, Rob helped launch 96744 United in Prayer, and served on the board of 808 United in Prayer. He also served as the chaplain of the Castle High School varsity baseball team for eight years.

Rob has been married to Barbara for thirty-two years and has three adult sons (Jordan, Brandon and Jonathan), two daughters-in-law (Stephanie and Michelle), and one granddaughter (Olivia).

Visit the author's website at www.familylegacyinternational.org

www.ingramcontent.com/pod-product-compliance
Lightning Source LLC
Chambersburg PA
CBHW031644040426
42453CB00006B/210